THE LORE OF
SAIL

THE LORE OF
SAIL

Facts On File Publications
460 Park Avenue South
New York, N.Y. 10016

THE LORE OF SAIL

Copyright©1982 by Nordbok, Gothenburg, Sweden.

Published in the United States of America in 1983 by
Facts on File, Inc., 460 Park Avenue South, New York, NY 10016.

Published in Sweden in 1983 by Nordbok, Gothenburg, Sweden.

Library of Congress Cataloging in Publication Data

Baker, William A.
  The lore of sail.

  Includes index.
  1. Sailing ships. I. Svensson, Sam II. Scheen,
Rolf III. Title.
VM145.B32 1984 623.8'223 83-1530

ISBN 0-87196-220-9

Printed in Spain 1983 by Novograph, S.A., Madrid

Contents

INTRODUCTION
by Sam Svensson

F rom ancient times, sailing the seas has been a unique profession, with techniques and methods which have always puzzled the landlubber. One thousand years before Christ, Solomon said that the way of a ship in the midst of the sea was too wonderful for him to understand.

In our time, there have been radical technical developments. On the seas, ships as well as the life of the sailor have been changed to such a degree that no similarity whatsoever with the olden days exists. This may be why general interest in old nautical things and in the sailing ship in particular has grown to such an extent. People all over the world now want accurate data about the construction, equipment, and handling of old ships.

Long ago, ships were always built of wood, except in the case of even more primitive materials such as reed, skin, and bark; but these materials were only used for the most primitive sailing in narrow seas. Since ancient times, ships have been built according to two methods: carvel and clinker. The first method was developed in the eastern Mediterranean countries, where Egyptians, Phoenicians, and others built ships with outside planking ingeniously joined by being placed edge to edge. This art came into general use in Southern Europe, and during the Middle Ages it spread along the coast of Western Europe, reaching the Baltic during the latter part of the 15th century. It then became the dominant way of shipbuilding, and after the middle of the 16th century all large vessels were carvel-built.

During the latter half of the 17th century, however, when shipbuilding had become a science and ships could be theoretically designed in advance, larger and sturdier ships were being built. The pictures on pages 33 and 34 show constructional details of a large 18th-century ship. During the second half of the 19th century, when iron and steel were being used more generally for shipbuilding, there was a decline in shipbuilding in wood. The art survived longest in the United States, where large wooden merchant sailing vessels were built up to the time of the First World War. The four-masted bark *Roanoke* – 3,439 gross tons, built in 1892 – and the six-masted schooner, *Wyoming* – 3,730 tons, built in 1909 – indicate the size limits of wood used in constructing ships. In many other places,

GRACE DIEU, also known as GREAT HARRY

perhaps mostly in the Eastern Mediterranean and in the Near East, but also in the Baltic, small sailing vessels were built of wood well into the 20th century. In addition to carvel-built wooden ships, clinker-built vessels were also being constructed. This method originated in the Baltic where, even during the Viking Age, large clinker-built ships sailed to Iceland and Greenland. In the Middle Ages, the clinker-building method was predominant in Northern Europe, and many large ships were constructed. Perhaps one of the largest was Henry IV's ship *Grace Dieu,* built in 1418; she was almost fifty meters long and about twelve meters wide. She had a complicated treble-clinker planking. According to the clinker method, the planking was built first and the frames were inserted afterward. We know this because the wreck of the *Grace Dieu* was discovered near Southampton, and it showed that the rivets of the skin were clinched underneath the frames.

Experimental ships of iron were built during the first half of the 19th century, until, gradually, iron came into more general use. After 1850, England had several shipyards which built only iron

GREAT BRITAIN was the first screw steamer built for transatlantic service. Designed by Brunel, she was built in 1843 of iron. She measured 289 ft. × 50 ft. and could accommo-date 360 passengers. She was later converted into a sailing ship. Her hull lay for many years in South Georgia. She is now restored in Bristol, where she was built.

vessels. The introduction of the steam engine for propulsion also encouraged the use of iron as a shipbuilding material. The first iron ships were built according to the same principles as those used for wooden vessels, but as builders grew more experienced, special methods were adopted for the structure of iron ships. One early change was to provide the iron steamship with a double bottom and internal keel, instead of the former bar keel used in sailing vessels. The keelson was now placed on top of the floors. Longitudinal framing, which slowly came into use around 1900, also deviated from the kind of standard ship-building that had been used for a thousand years.

The steam engine and later the diesel engine have only been in existence for a very short time in the whole history of naviga-tion. During most of this time, masts and sails were the only means of propulsion on long voyages. For ages, rigging con-sisted of one mast and one sail only, and it was not until the end of the Middle Ages that mechanical progress made it possible to construct better and more functional rigging. These develop-ments continued for several centuries and reached their high

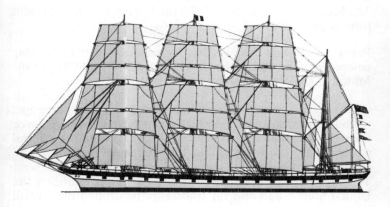

The steel-hulled ARCHIBALD RUSSELL was built in 1905, the last four-masted barque to be built for British owners (John Hardie of Glasgow). In 1924, she was sold to Gustaf Erikson of Mariehamn, Finland. At the outbreak of war in 1939, she was in Hull and was impounded by Britain. After the war, she was broken up.

point after the middle of the 19th century, when, due to competition from the steamship, shipyards turned out perfectly sparred and rigged sailing ships.

There have been many important phases in the history of rigging: such as setting a topsail above the original single square sail, using fidded topmasts that could be sent down, the footrope and the jackstay, which together revolutionized the work of handling sails, the introduction of wire, first for the standing rigging and then for the running gear, and, finally, mechanical aids for handling sails in large ships, such as patent sheaves and brace-and-halliard winches.

Flags are not only decorative but also useful. Originally, flags come from field banners carried in ancient battles. In comparison with the flags of ancient kings and military commanders, our national flags are of very recent date. The oldest national flag now in use is the Danish flag, according to a legend of 1219, and it was probably followed by the Swedish and Dutch flags. Among the flags of world powers, America has the oldest,

11

dating in its present general form of stars and stripes from 1777. The French tricolor is dated 1794; the English flag in its present form is from 1801.

Pages 210-211 show the flags used by some of the old sailing ship companies. The Hanseatic League's red-and-white flag of the Middle Ages comes as number one on this list.

Once the oar had been invented, there were very early attempts to find some mechanical aid which could move ships in a calm or drive them against a head wind. But there was no mechanical power. Thus, it was not until the steam engine was invented and perfected to some degree that steam navigation got under way. The first ships of this type were used for river traffic in the United States, and also for coastal traffic around the British Isles.

Deep-sea fishing is fun, but it is also an important means of getting food. Of old, deep-sea fishing was always carried out in fishing craft fitted with sails. Well-known examples of such craft are the English fishing smacks on the North Sea banks and the American schooners on the Newfoundland coast.

Sailing as a sport has an old heritage. Caligula had pleasure boats in Lake Nemi, and the Doge of Venice had a luxurious galley which he used every year in the ceremony of marrying himself to the sea. In ancient times, pleasure sailing was a sport reserved for kings and men of rank only. During the 19th century, it began to occupy more and more industrialists and businessmen, and, gradually, sailing as a sport has reached the widespread popularity of our own time. Today, there are yacht clubs in all countries where there is access to navigable waters. In order to standardize rules for yachting competitions, a great many so-called one-design boats have been constructed, boats which are built according to accurate measurements and regulations so that they will be exactly alike; thus it will be mostly the skill of the helmsman that decides the race. Yacht-racing courses are also decided according to an international standard.

As long as man has sailed the ocean, he has struggled for supremacy on the sea. Even in ancient times, a variety of ships were built specifically for war or trade; nevertheless, merchant ships have been used in war and warships in commerce down through the years. As the nations were industrialized, diversity according to function became more noticeable.

It might be said that navigation is the sailor's theory and seamanship his practice. The sounding lead is the sailor's oldest instrument; recognition of the coastline his only way of piloting. In deep waters and when land was out of sight this simple method of navigation was useless. Before the compass was invented, the sailor had to find his way by observations that would indicate a definite direction: the movement of the sun and stars, the direction of the wind and how the clouds were drifting, changes in ocean swell, the flight of birds and how the fish swam. On a long voyage not even the compass was a sufficient guide, so that such trips could not be undertaken until astronomic navigation had been discovered. Even then, for hundreds of years the only means by which a sailor could measure the sun's meridian height was with a simple instrument which determined latitude. The ability to make longitudinal calculations came at a much later date. For that purpose the navigator required Hadley's octant or a sextant, as well as a chronometer and complete nautical tables, or if there were no chronometer, he had to be able to calculate the longitude by means of lunar distances. As in other fields, electronics now does most of the work formerly done by astronomic navigation.

Previously, seamanship could be defined as the care and handling of sailing ships. Page 249 illustrates a portion of this almost forgotten art: how a brig can be put to sea against the wind by backing and filling downriver. Today, a vessel is guided by means of the rudder and the screw. The art of guiding a power-driven vessel has been mastered by many of today's seamen, but skill in sailing is rarely to be found. *The Lore of Sail* has tried to recover some small part of this forgotten art.

The first chapter of The Lore of Sail deals with the hull and some of its more im-portant details. The

next page shows a sketch of Columbus' ship, the SANTA MARIA.

THE HULL
by W.A. Baker

T hroughout history, the shape of ships' hulls has been determined by the materials and methods of construction, means of propulsion, use, fashion, and whim. Primitive craft still range in form from the round (woven baskets, skin-covered frameworks, and even pottery) to the long and narrow (bundles of reeds and shaped logs). Quite early on, the Egyptians sewed wooden planks together to produce flat-bottomed boats having the proportions of their reed craft. Other ancient peoples learned to improve the hollowed-out log canoe by spreading it open and adding one or more planks on each side. For centuries, built-up hulls followed the general shape of such canoes.

The continued existence of primitive craft in various parts of the world serves to emphasize the regions where major sea-going types of vessels developed – the Mediterranean basin, northern Europe, and China. Through most of recorded history, there was a parallel development of the two basic hull forms noted above, the "round" ship or bulky cargo carrier and the "long" ship built for speed. Shipbuilding history is concerned mainly with wooden oar-propelled and sailing vessels; metal ships and mechanical propulsion are relatively recent developments.

Two basic techniques have been employed in the construction of wooden vessels, the "shell" and the "skeleton", and combinations of them can be found as early as the 7th century. In the first, the planking is secured together and supporting frames added; in the second, as the term implies, a framework is erected to which the planking is fastened. The frames of a vessel built by the shell method take their shapes from the assembled planking while the planking of a skeleton-built ship must follow the predetermined shape of the frames. A possible explanation of the transition from the older shell technique to the skeleton is the retention in the hull of moulds erected to guide the shaping of the planking. Perhaps the earliest evidence of the skeleton method of construction is an early 14th-century painting showing Italian shipbuilders at work.

The features of early built-up vessels were the result of materials and tools employed. Early Scandinavian shipbuilders, for example, used the axe and adze to shape one long plank from each half of a split log. The planks so fashioned were lapped at the edges and secured together by withes or animal sinews (later by metal rivets); this is basically the present-day clinker planking. When a suitable number of planks had been fastened to each other and to the stem and sternpost, supporting frames were added which were held in place by lashings to lugs that had been left on the planks during the original shaping. Experts do not fully agree on the origin of the Viking ship. Some believe it developed from the skin boat when thin planks replaced sewn skins on a flexible framework but others favor the descent from the distended log canoe to which planks were added. The midsection of the famous Gokstad ship, *circa* 900 A.D., page 26, shows a late example of lashed-on planking; the lower eight planks were lashed to the frames while the upper planks were nailed.

Shipbuilders in ancient Egypt employed the saw to produce several planks from each log. The usual native woods, acacia and sycamore, were obtainable only in relatively short lengths which led Herodotus to liken the construction of an Egyptian ship to the building of a brick wall. In preserved vessels the planks were fastened edge to edge by various combinations of dowels or tenons, recessed dovetail pieces, and lashings which produced the smooth outside finish now called carvel planking. Being primarily river craft, Egyptian ships often had only a thick plank instead of a structural keel. Some types, built without frames, had arc-shaped midsections and were kept from spreading by deck beams that protruded through the planking. Large versions of Egyptian flat-bottomed boats had widely-spaced supporting frames and it is now believed that the larger round-bottomed vessels also had them. A prominent feature on many Egyptian vessels was a heavy rope truss, fitted from bow to stern, to keep the ends from drooping.

Available information indicates that Phoenician, Greek, and Roman ships were basically double-enders and that their builders, who employed the shell technique, had a sound knowledge of the structure needed in seagoing vessels. Records of numbers of Roman warships constructed in short periods of time, 220 ships in three months in 254 A.D., imply the use of some sort of moulds to achieve duplication of these shell-built vessels. The Romans had three basic types of vessels – chubby sailing merchantmen, stout warships propelled by oars and

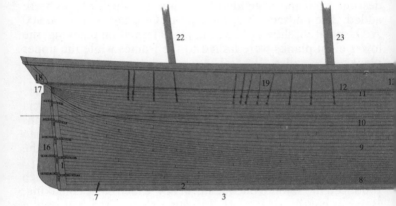

PROFILE OF A WOODEN SAILING SHIP, 1864

This semi-clipper ship was constructed in 1862 by Niels Kierkegaard, naval architect and Master Shipwright at the Old Shipyard in Gothenburg. In 1864, he published a handbook on naval architecture which contained drawings of eighteen different ships, includ-

ing this one. His example was followed by shipbuilders all over Scandinavia. The ship shown here has concave bows with narrow waterlines and a lean run under the transom counter and surmounting square stern. She was rigged as a bark, as indicated by the three shrouds

and single back stay in the mizzen rigging and shown by the chain plates. All the chain plates are bolted flat to the side of the ship without any channels. They go through the main rail, so the deadeyes will be located inside the topgallant bulwark. The fore and main

18

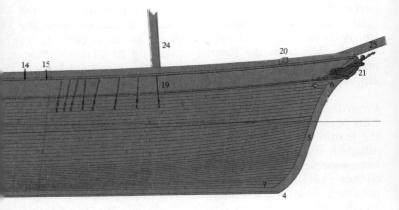

*rigging has four lower
shrouds, two topmast
backstays, one
topgallant backstay,
and one royal
backstay, as indicated
by the chain plates.
This same ship is
shown on pages 22
and 23.*

1 Sternpost
2 Keel
3 False keel or shoe
4 Fore foot, gripe
5 Stem
6 Headpiece
7 Garboard strake
8 Bottom planking
9 Side planking
10 Wale
11 Sheer strake
12 Covering board
13 Bulwark

14 Rough-tree rail
15 Topgallant bul-
wark
16 Rudder
17 Counter
18 Stern
19 Chain plates
20 Cathead
21 Figurehead
22 Mizzenmast
23 Mainmast
24 Foremast
25 Bowsprit

19

used for ramming in sea battles, and light speedy galleys for carrying messages and important persons.

From Roman times to about 1200 A.D., there was little change in the shapes of Mediterranean ships. The merchant sailing vessels remained double-enders with rather full sterns and they were still steered by heavy side oars. Following the earlier practice deck beam ends protruded through the carvel planking and were secured to heavy fore-and-aft wales. "Castles", not part of the hull, were fixed prominently on bow and stern, the light square work of house carpenters contrasting with the sturdy curved work of the shipwrights. One important change was the shift from the Roman square rig to a two-or-three-masted lateen rig for the majority of the merchant vessels, although the older rig continued to exist.

From the time of the first Crusade in 1095, when northern European vessels in large numbers entered the Mediterranean, the features of Northern and Southern "round" ships slowly mingled. By then, in the north, the typical Viking ships had been superseded by double-ended sailing vessels in which the clinker planking, high stem and sternpost, and side rudder persisted. These vessels became wider in proportion to length and deeper; they were fitted with a single deck supported inside the hull but a few heavy tie beams protruded through the planking. Small castles appeared on the bow and stern which became more substantial as time passed. Stern rudders were first used during the second half of the 12th century. Southern builders also adopted the stern rudder and returned to the square rig for their larger ships.

The more or less standard merchant ship type that resulted from the mingling of features, commonly called the cog, was employed from the Mediterranean to the Baltic into the early 15th century. The cog was basically a double-ender whose after body seems to have been fuller than her forebody. Her straight sternpost that carried the rudder had little rake; her stem, which had considerable rake forward, was usually straight in the north and curved in the south. The forecastle, triangular in plan, projected over the stem but its after end was partially faired into the hull. The stern castle was an angular house whose after corners overhung the sharp stern. The standard rig was one mast with a single square sail; the first addition to this rig seems to have been a lateen mizzen to improve steering balance. Still there were readily apparent differences between the Northern and Southern cogs. The former had clinker planking, a few projecting tie beams, and decks supported inside the hull, while cogs of the Mediterranean region had carvel planking with all deck beams protruding and secured to wales. Pictorial evidence for details of Northern cogs was substantiated in 1962 when a nearly complete 14th-century cog was found in the River Weser at Bremen.

Western historians, in concentrating their studies on the nations of the Mediterranean basin, tend to overlook the activities of Chinese seamen who from about 700 to 1500 A.D. probably were the world leaders in ocean shipping. There were well-documented voyages to Africa's east coast in the 14th and 15th centuries in ships that were about 200 feet long, had four or more masts, and carried complements of several hundred persons. There is a strong probability that Chinese ships sailed westward around the Cape of Good Hope and into the South Atlantic before 1459, nearly twenty years before the Portuguese rounded the Cape eastbound.

The origins of Chinese vessels are lost in time but it is thought that knowledge of shipbuilding was brought by colonists who came into China from the West. Some 20th-century types on the upper Yangtze River are practically identical with Egyptian craft of 1600 B.C. A Chinese treatise of 1119 A.D. likened the hull shape of the biggest ships to a rectangular grain measure that had sloping sides and ends and described a matting sail that moved around its mast like a door on a hinge. Marco Polo's descriptions of Chinese vessels at the end of the 13th century are well known; some information about Chinese ships may have reached Europe earlier through Arab traders. Far in advance of western technology, Chinese shipbuilders produced vessels with numerous transverse watertight bulkheads which are thought to have been inspired by the bamboo, centerline balanced rudders by the 1st century of our era, and leeboards by the mid-8th century. After the 15th-century African voyages official Chinese maritime activities were reduced to the minimum necessary to protect coastal shipping. Some types of vessels developed by that time probably have changed little

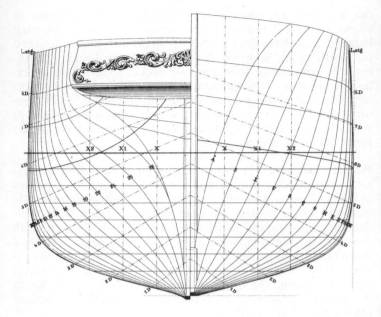

LINES OF A WOODEN SAILING SHIP OF 500 TONS DWT, 1864

The shape of the hull is determined by three sets of planes drawn at right angles to each other. Horizontal planes are called water lines, where they intersect the hull. They are shown as straight lines in A and as curves in B. WL indicates the load water line. Vertical planes going fore and aft and parallel to the longitudinal middle-line plane are called buttocks. Their intersections with the ship's hull are shown in A as curved lines, marked X, X1, and X2. Vertical planes going across the hull show the curves of the sides of the ship's transverse frame lines. Their shape is given in the body plan above, which shows an end view of the hull. The frame lines are numbered in the afterbody and lettered in the forebody. The body plan also gives the diagonal lines extending from the middle-line plane. The diagonal intersections with the surface of the hull are drawn (opposite) in C. D (opposite) gives the deck plan: three hatches, a fo'c'sle for 10 sailors, galley, and sail locker in the deckhouse, while the cabinhouse holds the captain's cabin, the mates' rooms, saloon, messroom, and pantries. The little house furthest aft holds the lamp locker and the officers' lavatory.

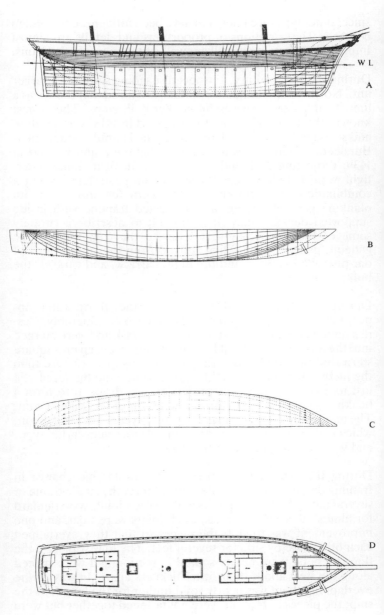

A

W L

B

C

D

since; other types are known to have been influenced by foreign contacts. The variations of proportions and details are almost impossible to catalog but all are well-suited to local conditions.

During the 15th century, European seagoing ships grew larger until Northern shipbuilders eventually realized that there was a limit to the size of successful clinker-built ships. The largest known, the *Grace Dieu* built in England in 1418, was a failure and sailed only from Southampton to the Hamble estuary near Bursledon where she was struck by lightning and burned in 1439. Projecting deck and tie beams, difficult to make watertight, were abandoned and the larger European ships became a combination of Northern and Southern features – smooth planking generally hung on pre-erected framing with inside supported decks. Today, it is difficult to describe accurately some of the ship types that followed the cog, such as the galleon, galleass, and galiot derived from the proportions of oar-propelled vessels, and the hulk, carrack, and caravel, the bulky cargo ships.

During the 15th and 16th centuries, the above-water appearance of European ships' hulls changed considerably. Castles remained large but lost their angular look and were merged into the main hull. Around 1550, large ships were given a square stern that provided better support to the superstructure than the medieval round stern. About the same time the forecastle lost its triangular form; its projection was dropped to form a beakhead below the bowsprit in imitation of the galley's ram. The major ship type for the next 75 to 100 years was the galleon, which had less sheer and lower superstructure than earlier types and was narrower in proportion to length.

During the 17th century, there was considerable change in framing details. Up to the late 16th century, the single frame of several naturally curved pieces with scarfed joints was standard for almost all sizes of vessels. Such joints were weak and one improvement was to shift the pieces so that they overlapped each other side by side for several feet. The lowest pieces, the floor timbers, were nearly square in section and were spaced along the keel about their own thickness apart. In way of the overlapping there was nearly solid timber for the length of the ship; the pieces of framing were not fastened together but were held in place by the outside planking and inside sheathing. By the early 18th century, the pieces had been extended to butt against each other and were fastened together to form complete frames that could be erected as units. This is essentially the pattern of framing still employed in the building of large wooden ships. Space does not permit descriptions of the various combinations of double full and single filling frames used in the intervening years.

The rough semicircular shape of the log canoe was poor for stability but builders soon learned that it could be improved by flattening the bottom of the log. In general, a flattened semicircle would be a simple description of the underwater midsection shape of nearly all vessels until the early part of the 18th century. The unusual V-shape of the Viking ships remained a local Scandinavian feature. Radical changes in the underwater forms of ships came in the 18th and 19th centuries.

The earliest preserved ship plans and treatises on shipbuilding date from the early 1400s. Written in Italian, they describe Mediterranean practices and indicate a long tradition of ship design using arcs of circles and their derivatives to shape hulls and their parts. Succeeding works from other countries amplify the details and show that hull proportions and parts were defined in terms of breadth or keel length, usually the former. Vessels built for fast sailing differed from bulky carriers more in relation of length to breadth than in the shape of the sections. In 1750, and perhaps even later, it was still possible to design a satisfactory ship with no tools but a pair of compasses and a straight-edge.

About 1670, the results of what perhaps were the first systematic ship resistance experiments were recorded in England. Other scientific studies followed, particularly in France, where the first treatise on stability was published in 1746.

In the 18th century, many legal and extra-legal operations required the use of small fast-sailing vessels. Those built first on Jamaica and later on Bermuda and the shores of Chesapeake Bay became world-famous. The terms Virginia-built or Virginia-model became almost synonymous with speed; by the early 19th century the type was known as the Baltimore clipper.

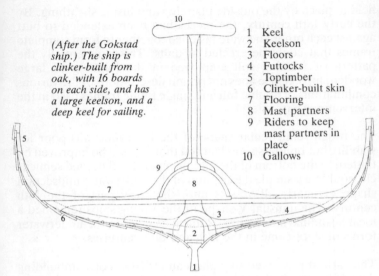

(After the Gokstad ship.) The ship is clinker-built from oak, with 16 boards on each side, and has a large keelson, and a deep keel for sailing.

1 Keel
2 Keelson
3 Floors
4 Futtocks
5 Toptimber
6 Clinker-built skin
7 Flooring
8 Mast partners
9 Riders to keep mast partners in place
10 Gallows

MIDSHIP SECTION OF A VIKING SHIP, MIDDLE OF 9TH CENTURY

The lower eight boards are tied to the ribs through cleats that are left on each board-plank. The rest of the boards are nailed. The ship is un-decked, but has a flat floor, on top of which a very heavy mast partner runs over six of the beams. The high gallows make it possible to erect a large tent on board. There are no rowing-benches. The oarsmen probably sat on loose benches or sea-chests.

(Opposite)
A *Wooden ship*
1 Keel
2 Garboard strake

3 Bottom planking
4 Bends or wales
5 Topside planking
6 Sheer strake
7 Floor
8 2nd futtock
9 4th futtock
10 Long toptimber
11 Limbers, water course
12 Keelson
13 Limber board
14 Limber strake
15 Floor ceiling
16 Thick strakes of ceiling
17 Air courses
18 Lower deck hanging knee
19 Lower deck shelf
20 Lower deck clamp
21 Hold stanchion
22 Lower deck beam

23 Lower deck, lower deck planking
24 Lower deck waterway
25 Lower deck spirketing
26 Tween deck ceiling
27 Upper deck hanging knee
28 Upper deck shelf
29 Upper deck clamp
30 Tween deck stanchion
31 Upper deck beam
32 Upper deck, upper deck planking
33 Upper deck waterway
34 Covering board
35 Bulwark stanchions
36 Planksheer

WOODEN AND WOOD AND IRON VESSEL

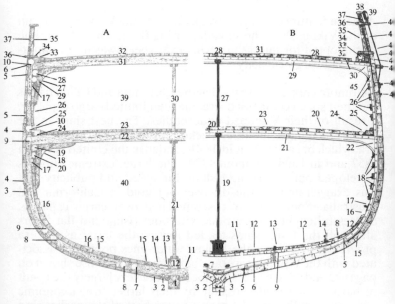

MIDSHIP SECTION OF TWO DIFFERENT SHIPS, SECOND HALF OF THE 19TH CENTURY

37	Bulwark planking	16	Covering board
38	Main rail	17	Bilge stringer
39	Tween decks	18	Cargo battens (in hold)
40	Hold	19	Hold pillar; hold stanchion
B	*Composite ship (wooden vessel with iron frames)*	20	Lower deck
		21	Lower deck beam
1	False keel or shoe	22	Bracket end (of lower deck beam)
2	Keel	23	Lower deck tie plate
3	Garboard strake	24	Lower deck stringer
4	Keel plate	25	Lower deck waterway
5	Frame	26	Cargo battens (between decks)
6	Floor	27	Upper deck pillar, upper deck stanchion
7	Limbers	
8	Reverse frame	28	Upper deck
9	Side intercostal keelson	29	Upper deck beam
10	Center line keelson	30	Bracket end (of upper deck beam)
11	Limber boards	
12	Ceiling	
13	Side keelson	
14	Bilge keelson	
15	Bilge plate	

31	Upper deck tie plate
32	Upper deck stringer plate
33	Upper deck waterway
34	Covering board
35	Bulwark stanchion
36	Main rail
37	Topgallant bulwark stanchion
38	Topgallant rail
39	Deadeye
40	Upper channel
41	Bulwark planking
42	Chainplate
43	Planksheer
44	Sheer strake
45	Iron sheer strake
46	Lower channel
47	Chain bolt
48	Preventer bolt

27

A major feature of the type was a return to the V-shaped bottom of the Viking ship, the so-called rising floor, which for a time was adopted for large ships whenever speed was more important than cargo capacity.

Baltimore clippers were tried in the East India and China trades but their speed could not overcome their limited cargo capacity, a result of their V-shaped underbodies. The best ships in the China trade had a modified packet ship form. The clipper ship era, which began in the mid-1840s, ended in the United States in 1857 and in England about 1870. The large, extreme clippers developed out of a rising fashion for speed and publicity that was exaggerated by the discovery of gold in California and Australia. Speed at any cost prevailed over cargo capacity. Successful clippers were built with both rising and flat floors although the faster ships tended toward the latter as the era progressed. Few had the hollow water-lines popularly associated with the type, the average being more like those shown on pages 22 and 23. Clipper ship speeds were very largely the result of hard driving made possible by their larger size. Economic pressures finally forced a return to the best of the packet ship forms, ships nearly as fast but capable of carrying more cargo.

The presence of figures of animals, gods, and goddesses on ships can be traced into antiquity; the latter two probably were used more to ensure divine protection than as decoration. The Vikings fitted fierce dragon heads on their ships to frighten their enemies. About 1600, there began a period of over a century of elaborate ship decoration on both merchant and warships in the form of stern and quarter galleries embellished with carvings, carved panels along the sides, large figureheads, and complicated head structures. By 1800, these had been reduced to some stern windows with a few carvings around them on the transom, small quarter galleries, and relatively simple head structures.

The introduction of successful commercial steam propulsion in the early 19th century brought new problems to shipbuilders – the concentrated weight of the machinery and the stresses induced by the paddle-wheels or the screw propeller. Until the end of their days, paddle-wheel steamers from European shipyards had their paddle-boxes constructed as appendages to

28

the hull. Except on ocean-going vessels builders in the United States carried the superstructures out to a line that enclosed the paddle-boxes.

Until about 1870, ocean-going steamships had the general form and construction of the sailing ship and, because of the unreliability of steam machinery, carried large sailing rigs. Sails for emergency use did not entirely disappear until nearly World War I.

By the middle of the 19th century, further resistance experiments and practical experience with steam propulsion had shown that fine lines were necessary for speed. A sailing ship could add sail to overcome poor lines, but early steam machinery was limited in power and breakdowns were frequent, occasionally with disastrous results.

Although a few iron parts had been used on wooden ships as far back as 1675, commercial iron shipbuilding did not start until the 1830s. Early practice was to have an iron structural member similar to every wooden part, which can be seen by comparing the sections shown on pages 27 and 30. Many shipowners were prejudiced against iron and before it was fully adopted there was the interim phase of the composite ship in which iron framing and tie plates were used with wood planking and decking, as shown on page 27.

As shipbuilders gained experience with iron vessels they learned that the longitudinal material could be distributed to better advantage than in wooden ships in which the keel was considered the backbone that provided most of the strength. It was soon realized that a metal ship should be built as a girder with as much strength in the deck as in the bottom. This, of course, is modern shipbuilding practice. Steel, which is now practically the universal material in all large ships, began to replace iron about 1870. Lightweight metals, particularly aluminium, are finding wide employment in the construction of superstructures on large ships and the entire hulls of yachts and other small vessels.

Chemical resins and glass fibers are now standard materials for the construction of yachts, small commercial craft, and even

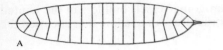

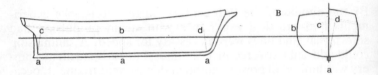

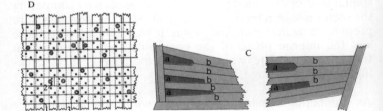

SOME CONSTRUCTION DETAILS OF WOODEN SHIPS, 19TH CENTURY

A The timbers were placed at right angles to the keel, except at the ends, both fore and aft, where they were placed at right angles to the ship's side. These frames were called cant timbers.

B To make the plank strakes run fair, fore and aft, the midship bend (ab) was divided into the same number of planks as the frames (ac) and as at the ends of the ship (ad).

C At the ends of the ship, if the planks were too wide, stealers (a) were put in between them; if too narrow, they were formed as joggle planks (b).

D Below the water line tree nails (trunnels) and bolts were used to fasten the planking to the frames in addition to two nails in each plank butt.

1 Tree nail
2 Bolt
3 Nail

WOODEN SHIP DETAILS

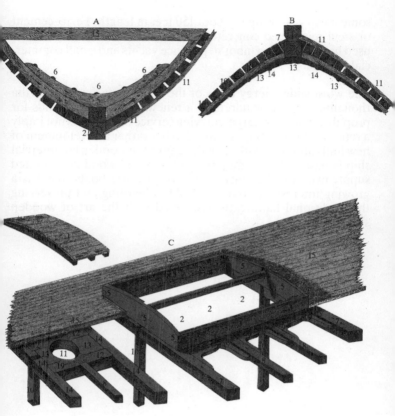

DETAILS OF A WOODEN VESSEL (FROM PAASCH)

A, B
   Horizontal
   section of bow
1 Stem
2 Stem rabbet
3 Apron
4 Eking
5 Deck hook
6 Deck hook bolts
7 Stem piece
8 Knight head
9 Hawse timbers
10 Fore cant timbers
11 Outside plank

12 Ceiling plank
13 Breast hook
14 Breast hook bolts
15 Deck beam
C *Deck and*
   hatchway
1 Hatch cover
2 Hatchway
3 Hatchway
   coamings
4 Hatchway carling
5 Head ledges
6 Fore and after
7 Hatch end beams

8 Half beams
9 Lodging knees
10 Deck stanchions
11 Mast hole
12 Mast carlings
13 Chocks
   (12 and 13
   forming
   mast partners)
14 Mast beams
15 Deck planking

some naval vessels up to about 150 feet in length. Ferro-cement or steel reinforced concrete is a low-cost material that can be used by semi-skilled labor to produce yachts and small commercial vessels.

The worldwide energy crisis of the early 1970s has turned the thoughts of some seafarers to a renewed use of the winds for propulsion in some cargo-carrying services. This does not imply a return to the old-time sailing ship but rather a development of new hulls and rigs. Although the day of the wooden commercial ship is past and in some parts of the world wood is in limited supply even for the construction of pleasure boats, there is a growing interest by young and old in learning and preserving the traditional handcrafts associated with the art of wooden shipbuilding.

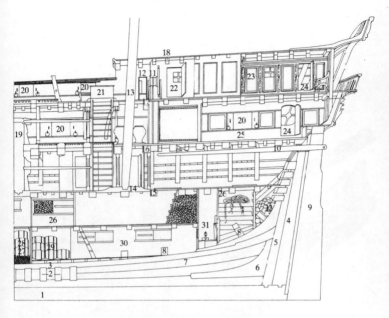

LONGITUDINAL SECTION OF THE AFTERBODY OF A 40-GUN FRIGATE, 1768

1 Keel	13 Mizzenmast	24 Doorway to
2 Floors	14 Mast step	quarter gallery
3 Keelson	15 Orlop deck beams	25 Wardroom
4 Sternpost	16 Gun deck beams	26 Storerooms
5 Inner post	17 Upper deck	27 Ballast
6 Stern knee	beams	28 Water, beer casks
7 Deadwood	18 Poop deck beams	29 Salt meat
8 Crutches	19 Main capstan	30 Powder room
9 Rudder	20 Gunports	31 Lantern for
10 Tiller	21 Companion hood	powder room
11 Wheel	22 Officer's room	32 Shot locker
12 Binnacle	23 Great cabin	

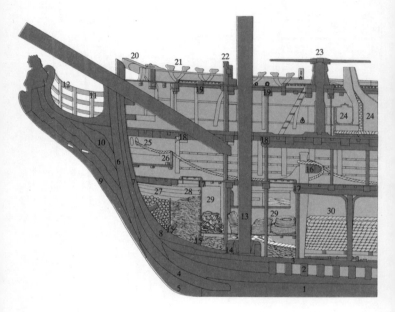

LONGITUDINAL SECTION OF THE FOREBODY OF A 40-GUN FRIGATE, 1768

1	Keel	12	Head rails	21	Kevels
2	Floors	13	Foremast	22	Knight
3	Keelson	14	Mast step	23	Jeer capstan
4	Forefoot	15	Breast hooks	24	Galley
5	Gripe	16	Bitts	25	Cable
6	Stem	17	Orlop deck	26	Mangerboard
7	Apron		beams	27	Shotlocker
8	Stemson	18	Gun deck beams	28	Galley wood
9	Bobstay piece	19	Upper deck	29	Bosun's stores
10	Filling chocks		beams	30	Cable tier
11	Head timbers	20	Cathead		

THREE-MASTED BARK

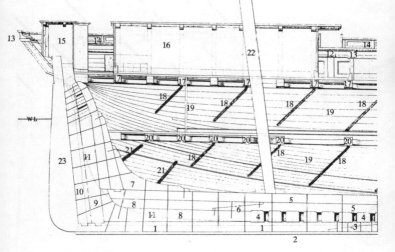

THREE-MASTED BARK, LONGITUDINAL SECTION OF THE AFTERBODY

1	Keel	12	Pinrail	19	Ceiling
2	False keel or shoe	13	Main rail	20	Tween deck
3	Keel scarf	14	Topgallant bul-		beams
4	Floor		wark	21	Crutches
5	Keelson	15	Lamp locker,	22	Mizzenmast
6	Keelson scarf		roundhouse	23	Rudder
7	Stern knee	16	Cabin house		
8	After deadwood	17	Main deck beams		
9	Inner post	18	Diagonal deck		
10	Sternpost		beam		
11	Bearding line		hanging knees		

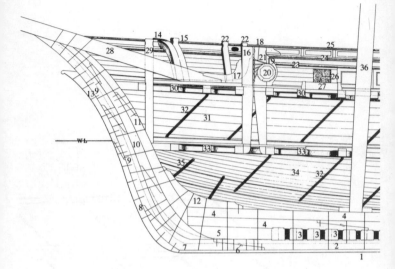

THREE-MASTED WOODEN SHIP, 500 TONS DWT, LONGITUDINAL SECTION OF THE FOREBODY

1 False keel or shoe	15 Kevel head	28 Bowsprit
2 Keel	16 Pawl bitt	29 Foreward bitt
3 Floors	17 Standard knee	30 Main deck beams
4 Keelson	18 Pawls	31 Tween deck
5 Fore deadwood	19 Pawl rim	ceiling
6 Keel scarf	20 Windlass barrel	32 Main deck
7 Fore foot	21 Carrick bitt or	diagonal hanging
8 Cutwater piece,	windlass bitt	knees
gripe	22 Mooring bollards	33 Tween deck
9 Stem	23 Pinrail	beams
10 Apron	24 Main rail	34 Lower hold
11 Stemson	25 Topgallant rail	ceiling
12 Stem knee	26 Port	35 Breast hooks
13 Lace piece	27 Fore hatch	36 Foremast
14 Cathead	coaming	

CARPENTER'S TOOLS

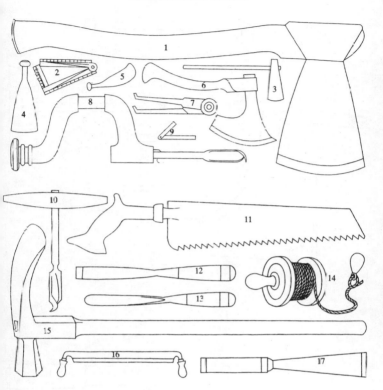

CARPENTER'S TOOLS, 1691

1 English broad axe
2 Folding rule, a
   foot and a half
   long
3 Horse iron with
   an iron handle
4 Reeming iron
5 Curved caulking
   iron
6 Carpenter's
   hatchet
7 Inside calipers
8 Dutch brace and bit
9 Small bevel
10 English auger with
   a screw

11 Dutch handsaw
12 English chisel
13 Gouge
14 Chalk line and
   reel
15 English adze
16 Draw knife
17 Chisel with a
   handle

CARPENTER'S TOOLS

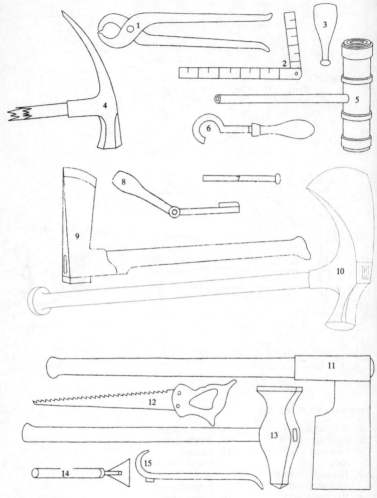

CARPENTER'S TOOLS, 1691

1 Pair of pincers
2 Dutch rule
3 Caulking iron
4 Adze, as seen from the side
5 Big mallet with iron hoops
6 Crab iron
7 Spike iron
8 Crab iron, made like a clasp knife
9 Swedish chopping axe
10 Swedish adze
11 Dutch axe
12 Compass saw
13 Sledge hammer
14 Deck scraper
15 Rave hook or ripping iron for cleaning caulking from seams
16 English handsaw

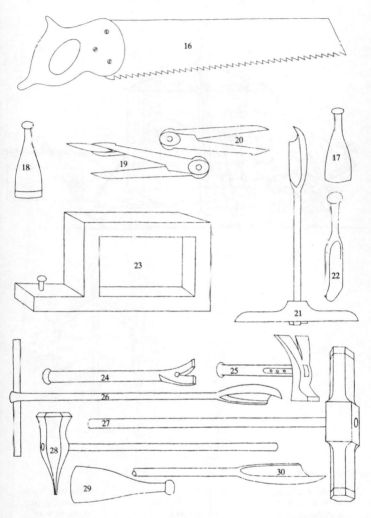

17 Caulking iron
18 Making iron
19 Compasses with crayon
20 Dividers
21 Swedish auger
22 Small gouge to start auger holes

23 Grease well to use when caulking
24 Crowbar
25 English claw hammer
26 English auger with a wooden handle

27 English caulking mallet
28 Common hammer
29 Reeming iron
30 Swedish gouge for pinewood

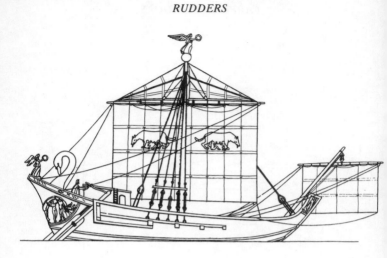

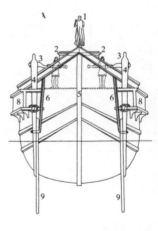

ANCIENT RUDDERS

A   *Rudder arrange-ment in a Roman merchant ship about A.D. 200*
1   Stern ornament
2   Helmsmen
3   Tillers
4   Rudder stock
5   Sternpost
6   Carrying ropes
7   Lashing

8   Balcony
9   Rudder blade
B   *Tiller of the Vik-ing ship from Gokstad, about A.D. 850*
C   *Rudder arrange-ment in the Vik-ing era (Gokstad ship)*

1   Broadside view of steering oar
2   Stern view of steering oar
3   Tiller
4   Rudder rope
5   Knot
6   "Wart"
7   Tilting rope
8   Collar

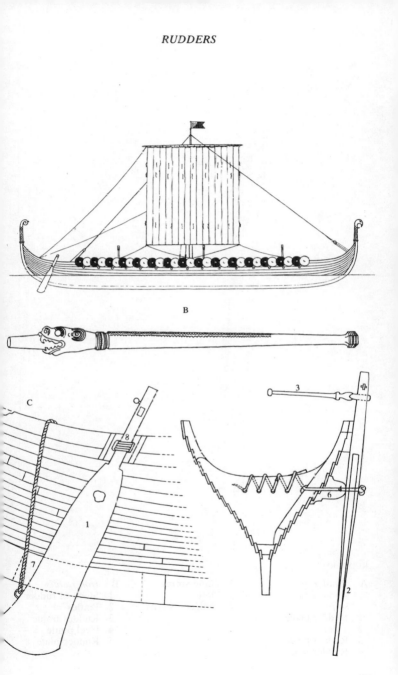

B

C

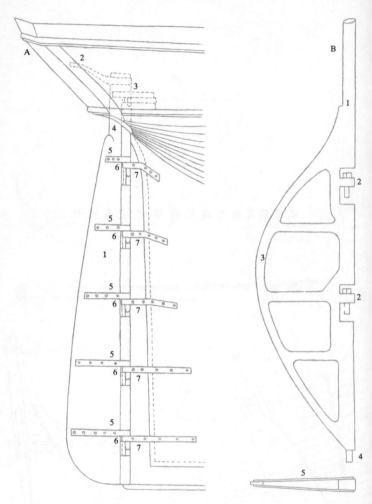

RUDDERS

A *Rudder in a wooden sailing ship*
1 Rudder blade
2 Tiller
3 Rudder head
4 Rudder stock

5 Pintle straps
6 Pintles
7 Gudgeon straps

B *Iron rudder*
1 Stock of rudder
2 Pintles
3 Rudder frame
4 Heel pintle
5 Rudder plate

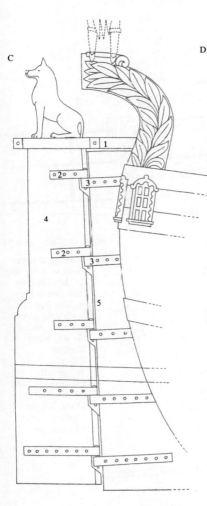

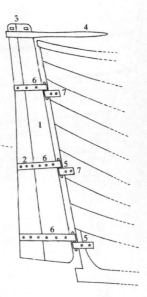

C *Rudder of a Dutch fleut, middle of 17th century*
1 Tiller
2 Pintle straps
3 Rudder braces or gudgeon straps
4 Rudder blade
5 Sternpost
D *Rudder of small medieval ship*
1 Main piece of rudder
2 Back piece
3 Head
4 Tiller
5 Pintles
6 Pintle straps
7 Gudgeon straps

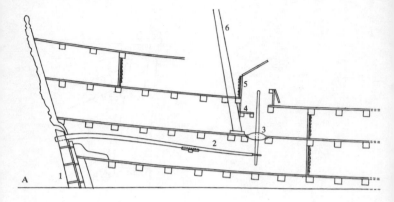

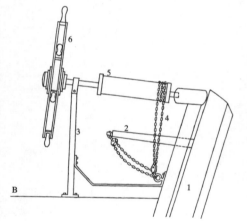

SOME STEERING GEARS

A *Steering arrangement in a big ship of the 17th century, when the rudder was controlled by a vertical lever called the whipstaff*
1 Rudder
2 Tiller
3 Whipstaff
4 Platform for the quartermaster
5 Hood for the quartermaster
6 Mizzenmast

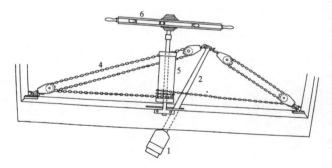

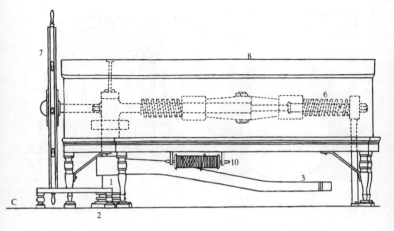

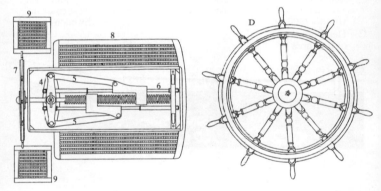

B *Common steering gear in elevation and plan of small wooden sailing ship, 19th century*
1 Rudder
2 Tiller
3 Wheel stand
4 Tiller chain
5 Barrel or drum
6 Wheel
C *Mechanical screw steering gear in plan and eleva-*

tion of big steel sailing ship, latter part of 19th century
1 Rudder stock
2 Stuffing box on deck
3 Emergency tiller
4 Cross head
5 Coupling rods
6 Screw spindle-threaded right and left
7 Wheel

8 Wheel box with side seats
9 Wheel gratings
10 Log reel slung underneath wheel box

D *Steering wheel from sailing ship, middle of the 19th century*

45

A The flower of the English hawthorn on the

Mayflower, 1620 (from replica built in 1957)

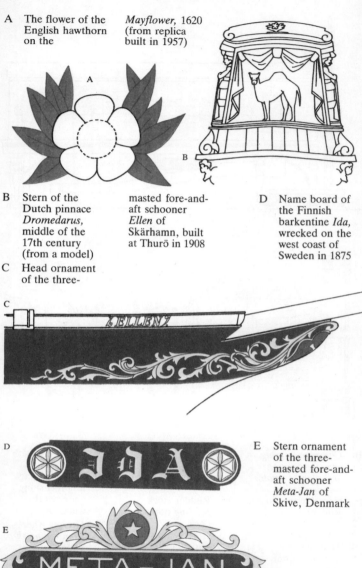

B Stern of the Dutch pinnace *Dromedarus,* middle of the 17th century (from a model)

C Head ornament of the three-

masted fore-and-aft schooner *Ellen* of Skärhamn, built at Thurö in 1908

D Name board of the Finnish barkentine *Ida,* wrecked on the west coast of Sweden in 1875

E Stern ornament of the three-masted fore-and-aft schooner *Meta-Jan* of Skive, Denmark

DECORATION

*With most people il-
literate, the name of a
ship was often
depicted by painted
carvings on the stern
(for example A and B)*

Stern of the
French ship *Le
Soleil Royal*,
built at Brest in
1669

LE SOLEIL ROYAL

47

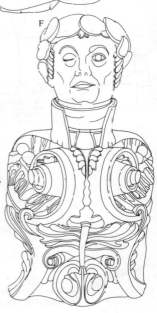

FIGUREHEADS AND
CARVINGS

A   *Unidentified
    wood carving, c.
    1820*
B   *Figurehead of
    unknown vessel,
    from the middle
    of the 19th cen-
    tury*
C   *Name-board of
    the* ALBION, *19th
    century*
D   *Unidentified
    figurehead, c.
    1850*

E   *Unidentified car-
    ving, c. 1850*
F   *Figurehead of the*
    HORATIO, *1807*

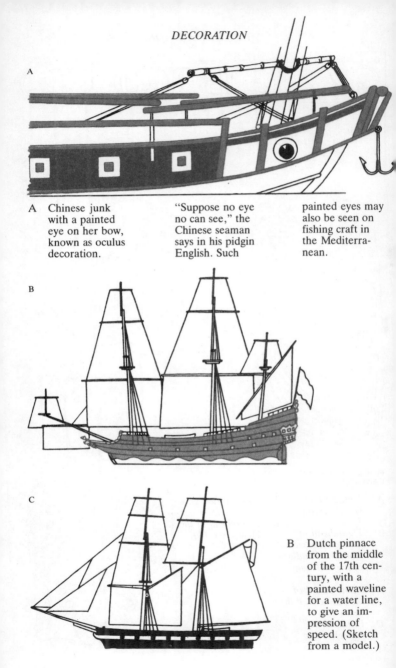

A Chinese junk with a painted eye on her bow, known as oculus decoration.

"Suppose no eye no can see," the Chinese seaman says in his pidgin English. Such painted eyes may also be seen on fishing craft in the Mediterranean.

B Dutch pinnace from the middle of the 17th century, with a painted waveline for a water line, to give an impression of speed. (Sketch from a model.)

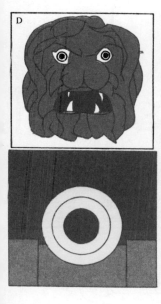

C Brigantine from the middle of the 19th century, with painted ports on her sides. This painting was originally intended to make the ship look like a man-of-war, but later it remained as decoration only.

D Sculptured lion's head on gun-port lid, perhaps intended to put heart in the crew and to frighten the enemy: the Swedish ship *Wasa,* 1628

E Figurehead, from the 18th century

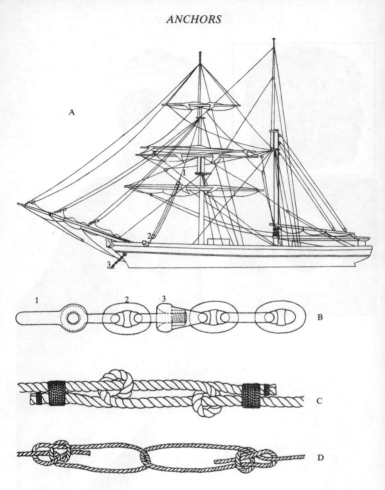

ANCHORS AND ANCHOR GEAR

A *Arrangement for fishing an anchor*
1 Pendant with fish tackle
2 Cathead
3 Chain cable
B *Chain cable*
1 Shackle
2 Stud link
3 Swivel

C, D *Hawser bends*
E *Grapnel*
F *Iron-stocked anchor*
G *Trotman's anchor*
H *Inglefield's anchor*

I *Cathead with anchor gear*
1 Anchor
2 Cable
3 Shackle
4 Cathead
5 Releasing gear
6 Cathead stopper
J *Mushroom anchor*
K *Hall's anchor*

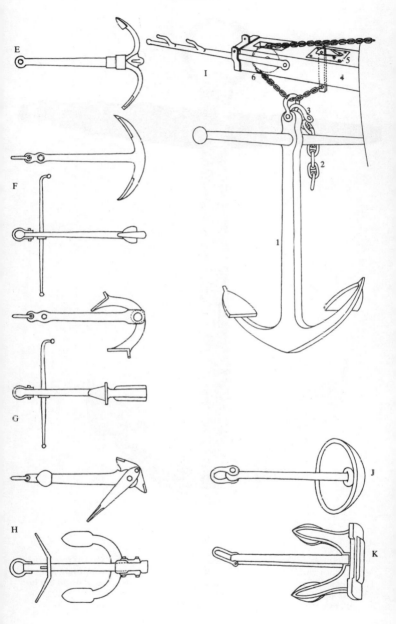

ANCHORS

ANCHORS

A *Common anchor*
1 Anchor ring
2 Stock
3 Hoops of the
   anchor stock
4 Shank
5 Crown
6 Arm
7 Fluke
8 Pea or bill

B *Part of tree trunk
   with branches,
   used as an anchor*

ANCHORS

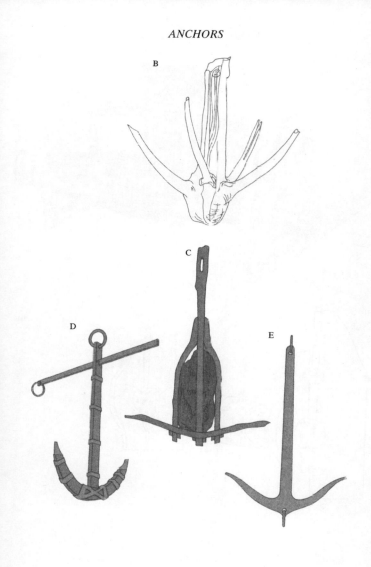

C Anchor, made from tree branches and stone

D Roman anchor of Caligula from Lake Nemi

E Viking anchor from the Oseberg ship

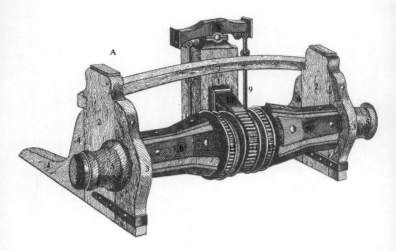

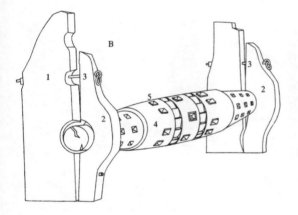

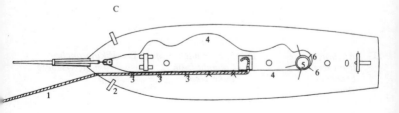

WINDLASS AND CAPSTAN

A *Windlass*
1 Pawl bitt
2 Windlass bitts
3 Cheeks of
  windlass bitts
4 Standard knees
5 Warping heads
6 Windlass barrel
  with whelps
7 Strongback
8 Crosshead
9 Purchase rod
10 Pawl
11 Pawl rim
12 Purchase rims

B *Old windlass*
1 Windlass bitt
2 Cheek of
  windlass bitts
3 Bolts
4 Windlass barrel
5 Bar holes

C *Method of heav-
  ing anchor with a
  messenger*
1 Cable
2 Cathead
3 Nippers
4 Messenger (an
  endless rope)
5 Capstan
6 Capstan bars

D *Capstan*
1 Head
2 Bar holes
3 Barrel
4 Whelps

E *Capstan*
1 Drumhead
2 Capstan-bar
  holes
3 Barrel
4 Whelps
5 Whelp chocks
6 Pawls
7 Pawl rim
8 Capstan partners
9 Deck planking

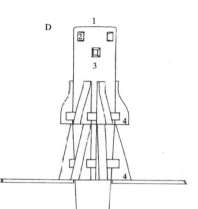

57

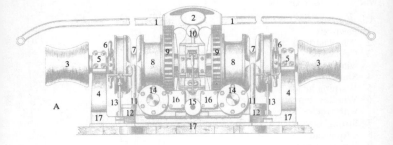

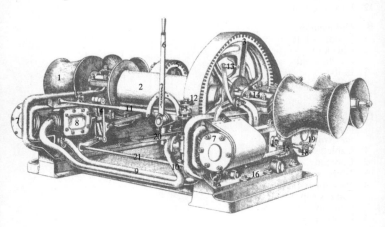

WINDLASS AND WINCH

A *Patent steam windlass*
1 Levers, hand-power levers
2 Crosshead
3 Warping heads
4 Side bitts
5 Bearing caps
6 Screwbrake nuts
7 Wildcats (Gypsies)
8 Windlass barrel or drum
9 Main cone driving wheels
10 Crosshead bracket
11 Cable relievers
12 Chain pipes
13 Bandbrakes
14 Cylinders
15 Steampipe flange
16 Valve casings
17 Bedplate

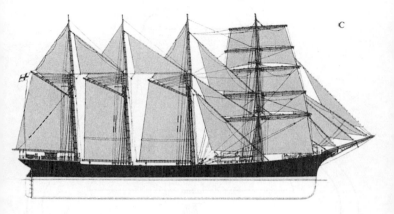

C

B *Steam winch*
1 Warping heads or gypsy heads
2 Winch drum
3 Main cogwheel
4 Reversing link
5 Pinion shaft cogwheel
6 Clutch lever
7 Cylinders
8 Slide-valve box
9 Steam exhaust pipe
10 Inlet steampipe
11 Tie rod, stay
12 Throttle valve
13 Reversing lever
14 Drum shaft bearing
15 Connecting rod
16 Bedplate
17 Piston rod and crosshead
18 Crank pin
19 Combined gear- and flywheel
20 Strap-brake pedal
21 Weigh shaft

C *The four-masted barquentine* MOZART, *built in 1904 at Greenock for German ownership. Her registered dimensions were 260 ft.×40.5 ft. and she had a gross tonnage of 2,005. She was very up-to-date in design, and besides being fitted with water ballast tanks, she was given such labour-saving devices as halliard and brace winches, steam-powered by a donkey boiler. In 1922, she was sold to Hugo Lundguist of Mariehamn, Finland, and she spent her last years sailing the Australian route. She was broken up in 1936.*

A

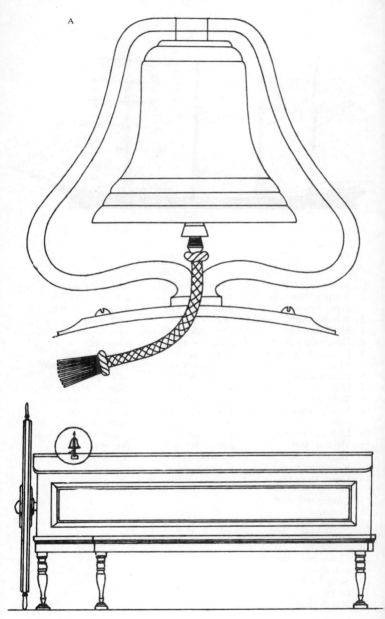

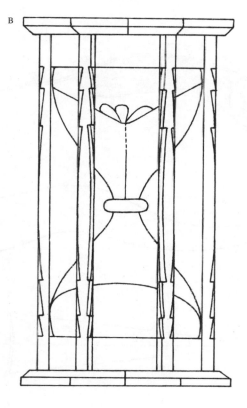

BELL AND HOURGLASS

A A little bell placed aft, on which the helmsman struck the time, and which was repeated by the lookout at the main bell

B Hourglass, measuring half an hour. Each glass on board accounts for half an hour, and is sounded by one stroke of the bell; each watch of four hours is divided into eight glasses, corresponding to eight bells. The six watches are: the 1st watch 20–24, the 2nd watch (middle watch) 00–04, the day watch (morning watch) 04–08, the forenoon watch 08–12, the noon watch 12–16, and the afternoon watch 16–20. Three bells thus mean that the time is 01.30, 05.30, 09.30, 13.30, 17.30, or 21.30. Eight bells mean that a watch is over. The number of glasses is struck on the bell as a series of double strokes. For instance, 15.30 (seven glasses): ++ ++ ++ +

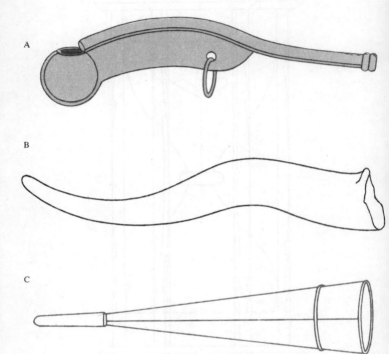

WHISTLES AND BELL

A Boatswain's call
B Fog horn made from a bullock's horn
C Fog horn of copper
D A bell hanging in a belfry, Nelson's VICTORY
E Admiral Nelson's flagship at Trafalgar, 1805, was VICTORY, launched in 1765. She was a first-rate ship of the line with three gun-decks and 102 guns. Her crew totalled 850 men. She is one of the few preserved wooden warships in Great Britain, where she lies at Portsmouth.

D

E

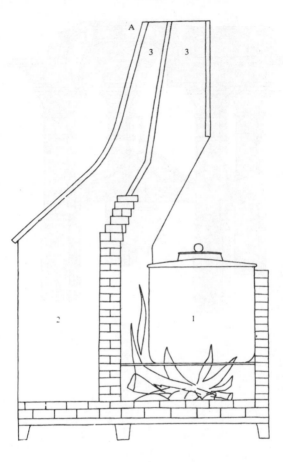

GALLEY

A *Ship's galley, according to Chapman, 1768*
1 Pea-soup kettle
2 Brick fireplace
3 Galley stacks

B *Brick fireplace on board the Swedish ship Wasa, 1628. There was no chimney and the smoke had to find its way out wherever it could.*

C *Open sheet-iron fireplace, on the deck of a coaster in the Indian Ocean*

D *Big galley stove, from the beginning of the 20th century*

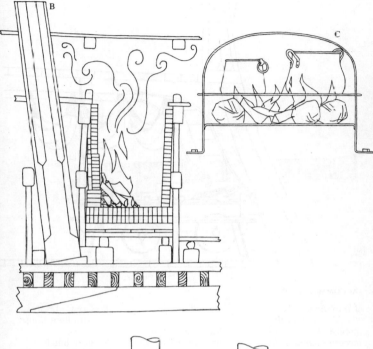

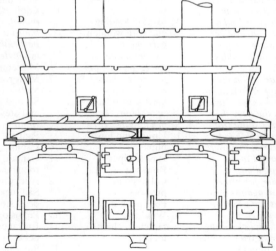

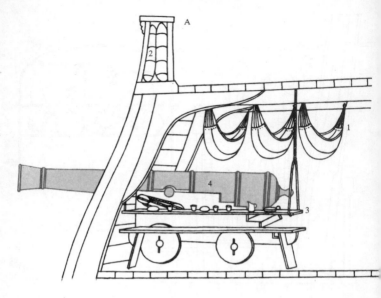

ACCOMMODATIONS

Up to the middle of the 17th century the crew had no special accommodations but had to sleep on the bare deck or find a place for themselves. Meals were eaten on deck without tables or chairs.

A *Early 19th century. When hammocks were used in the navy they were slung from the deck-head beams; they were stowed in the topgallant bulwark for protection against musket fire when not in use*

1 Hammocks slung under deck beams
2 Hammocks

stowed in bulwark
3 Mess table slung from overhead beam
4 Muzzle-loading gun with wooden carriage

B *Accommodation for 12 seamen in fo'c'sle on board a British three-masted iron bark of 900 tons, built in Glasgow, 1879*

1 Upper and lower bunks
2 Hawse pipes
3 Bowsprit
4 Cable compressors
5 Fore peak hatch
6 Windlass
7 Hatch to chain locker

8 Crew's lavatory with light house above
9 Fore hatch

C *Cabin accommodations on board a Swedish barkentine, built in Gävle, 1878*

1 Mizzenmast
2 Mess room
3 Mate's room
4 Second mate's and steward's room
5 Pantry
6 Cabin
7 Captain's bedroom
8 Alleyway
9 Sail locker and deck stores
10 Provisions
11 Entrance from deck
12 Steering compass

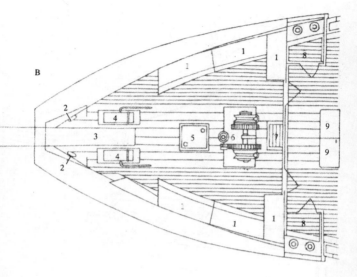

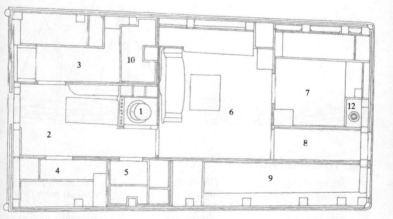

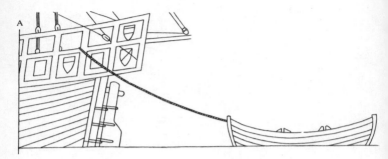

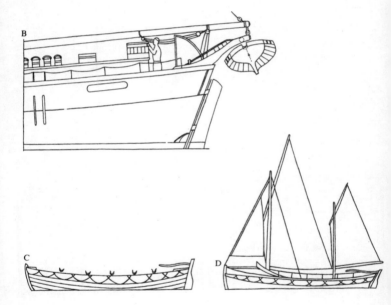

SOME TYPES OF LIFEBOAT

A   *Medieval ship
    towing her barge*
B   *Auxiliary coaster
    with her boat
    slung from short
    davits across her
    transom stern*

C   *Old pulling
    lifeboat*
D   *English sailing
    lifeboat, about
    1900*
E   *Norwegian cruis-
    ing lifeboat,* COL-
    IN ARCHER. *1893*

F   *British self-righting
    lifeboat from 1960*
G   *Modern
    fiberglass lifeboat*

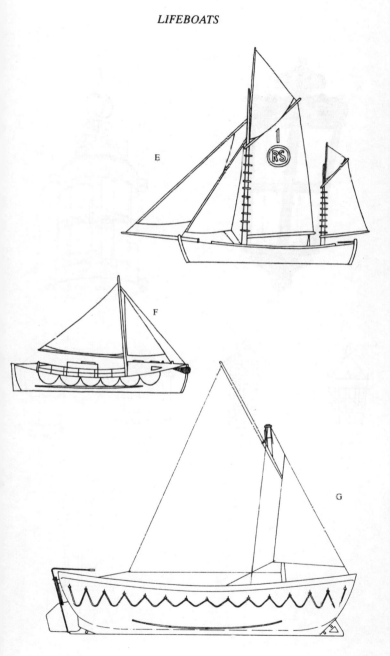

LANTERNS

A

B

C 1

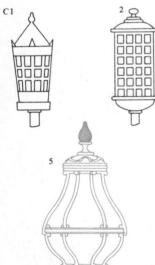

2

3

4

5

6

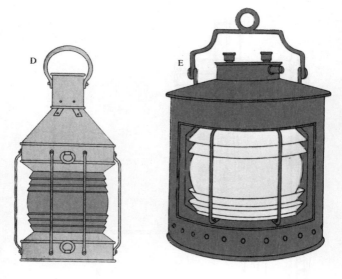

LANTERNS AND SIDELIGHTS

A *Swedish poop lantern from the 18th century*
B *Lantern with horn windows from the 18th century*
C *Development of the poop lantern*
1 1514, *Great Harry*
2 Middle of the 16th century, Sir Francis Drake's *Golden Hind*
3 The 17th century. Dutch poop lantern
4 The 17th century. English poop lantern, *Prince Royal*
5 The 18th century, poop lantern of a big

French ship, built at Brest in 1756
6 The 18th century, Swedish poop lantern (same as A)
D *Riding light with a round wick lamp and Fresnel lens (A.J. Fresnel, French physicist, 1788–1827)*
E *Sidelight for kerosene, paraffin oil, from the beginning of the 20th century*
F *Starboard side light house on board big sailing ship, the 19th and 20th centuries*

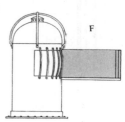

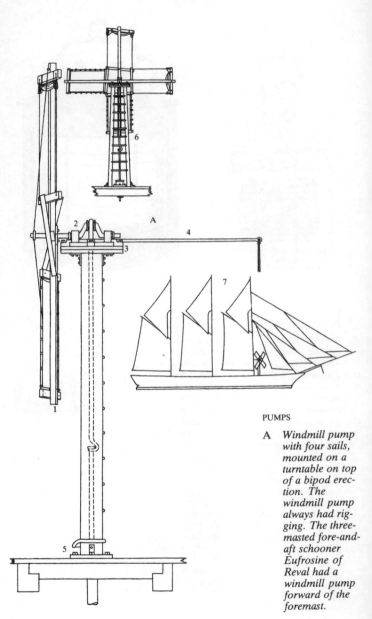

PUMPS

A   *Windmill pump
with four sails,
mounted on a
turntable on top
of a bipod erec-
tion. The
windmill pump
always had rig-
ging. The three-
masted fore-and-
aft schooner
Eufrosine of
Reval had a
windmill pump
forward of the
foremast.*

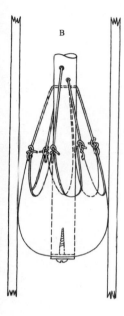

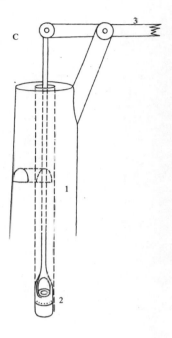

1 Sails as seen from the side
2 Crankshaft
3 Turntable
4 Arm with braces, for setting the mill to the wind
5 The pump deck seating
6 Front view of windmill, showing two sails furled and two set
7 Three-masted fore-and-aft

schooner with a windmill pump

B *Old-type bilge pump, once common in small craft in the Baltic area. It was constructed from a piece of leather, which formed a bag, and gave good service.*

C *The standard bilge pump in small wooden sailing vessels. It was made from a straight tree trunk, bored through the heart.*
1 Trunk of pump
2 Pump bucket
3 Pump brake, handle

SPARS AND RIGGING
By Sam Svensson

E xactly when and where primitive man first rigged a mast and sail to his simple boat remains a mystery. But quite early, he must have noticed that if he stood up in his craft, he would drift in the direction in which the wind was blowing. If he wanted to go in this direction, he might very well have speeded up his journey by holding up a cloak or animal hide to catch the wind. The time that elapsed between this first step and the introduction of the first real mast was certainly extremely long. And for many thousands of years, a single mast and a simple square sail were the limit of the ancient sailor's ability to rig a boat.

Far along through the ages, from the Old Empire in Egypt and well into the European Middle Ages, the single mast remained the only rig. One break in the monotony comes in the Roman era, when the Roman sailing ship had a bowsprit, sometimes seen as a greatly inclined foremast.

In Mediterranean lands, where the rowing galley played an important role, the mast and sail evolved somewhat differently than in Western Europe, where the single mast and square sail were prevalent up to the beginning of the 15th century. The standing rigging was very simple. Smaller ships at times had none, as in the rudimentary sailing boats of the early Scandinavian fishermen.

The running gear also was very simple. The halliard hoisting the sail was led aft and acted as a backstay, thus also serving to strengthen the mast when sailing. In the early Middle Ages bowlines were added to the sail and led forward to a spar, called the bowsprit, which was rigged out over the stem.

The shrouds were set up with deadeyes and lanyards, and the rigging was rattled down, forming rope ladders to facilitate going aloft. The Northern ship was also given a fighting top at the masthead. This top is actually very old. In fact, our oldest reproduction of the fighting top is to be found on an Egyptian relief from about 1200 B.C. The oldest top mentioned in Scandinavia is in the saga of Haakon Hardabred, 1159, contained in *Snorres Konungasagor.*

76

Sometime during the first half of the 15th century, larger ships were built with two or three masts. In Northwest Europe evolution quickly culminated in three masts. The mainmast kept its location in the middle of the ship, and from the beginning, the new masts were stepped in the fore- and aftercastles. It was most likely that flags or banners were first flown there, a common practice during the Crusades, and that it was just as easy to hoist a small sail on this same flagpole. One could even go so far as to say that every square sail, except the first, of course, was preceded by a flag on a pole. Thus, big ships unfurled a banner aloft on a staff in the fighting top, and toward the end of the 15th century, they appeared with a small sail on the same staff. From the beginning this small sail was handled by the men in the top, and it was from this that the name topsail was derived. The Dutch, Germans, and Scandinavians used a similar term; to them the sail was known as the "märssegel." The main topsail was soon followed by a second sail on the foremast. Both were small at first, but they continually increased in size as they came to be used more and more. The clews were sheeted to the yardarms below, and, with braces and clewlines leading down to the deck, the sail became more functional. As it could be set flatter, it could be used when sailing on the wind.

The triangular lateen sail, in general use in galleys and fishing boats of the Mediterranean, was eventually used as the mizzen in big ships all along the European coast. Its use had spread all the way to the Baltic Sea by the end of the Middle Ages. There, it gradually supplanted the older square sail as the mizzen. In the 250 years that followed, the lateen mizzen continued to be used in all larger ships.

The bowsprit had originally served only to lead the bowlines. By the end of the Middle Ages, however, a square sail had been rigged under the bowsprit. This sail was called a blind in Medieval English, as it wholly blocked the view ahead. It was, perhaps, the blind that prompted the need for a lookout aloft. Later, it became known as the spritsail.

By the last quarter of the 15th century, larger ships began to have as many as four masts. The two aftermost masts generally had lateen sails only, but the main mizzenmast could carry a triangular topsail on a topmast as well. The smaller mizzen,

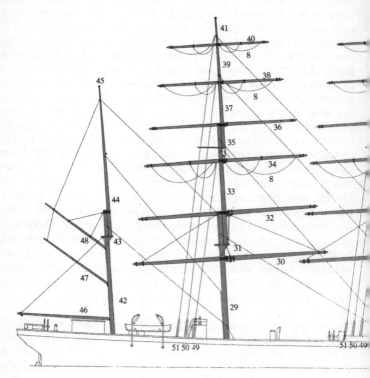

SPARS OF A FOUR-MASTED BARK

1	Spike bowsprit	11	Fore topgallant mast	19	Main lower top-sail yard
2	Fore lower mast	12	Fore upper topgallant yard, hoisted	20	Main topmast
3	Fore yard			21	Main upper top-sail yard, hoisted
4	Fore top	13	Fore royal mast in one with topgallant mast	22	Main topmast crosstree
5	Fore lower top-sail yard			23	Main lower topgallant yard
6	Fore topmast	14	Fore royal yard, hoisted	24	Main topgallant mast
7	Fore upper top-sail yard, hoisted	15	Fore royal pole	25	Main upper topgallant yard, hoisted
8	Lifts	16	Main lower mast		
9	Fore topmast crosstree	17	Mainyard		
10	Fore lower topgallant yard	18	Main top		

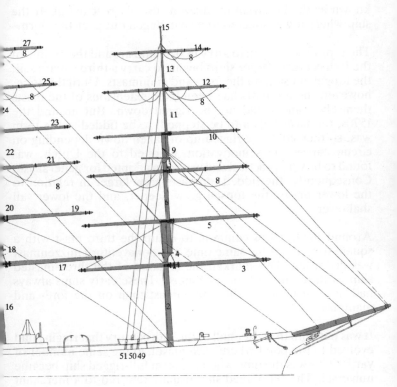

26	Main royal mast	35	Mizzen topmast	42	Jigger lower mast
27	Main royal yard, hoisted		crosstree	43	Jigger top
28	Main royal pole	36	Mizzen lower topgallant yard	44	Jigger topmast
29	Mizzen lower mast	37	Mizzen topgallant mast	45	Jigger pole
30	Crossjack yard	38	Mizzen upper topgallant yard, hoisted	46	Spanker boom
31	Mizzen top			47	Lower spanker gaff
32	Mizzen lower topsail yard	39	Mizzen royal mast	48	Upper spanker gaff
33	Mizzen topmast	40	Mizzen royal yard, hoisted	49	Upper topsail halliard
34	Mizzen upper topsail yard, hoisted	41	Mizzen pole	50	Upper topgallant halliard
				51	Royal halliard

79

known as the bonaventure mizzen, usually reached abaft the ship where it was sheeted to a spar rigged out over the stern.

The topsail continued to grow in size, and around the middle of the 16th century, larger ships began to carry a third square sail, the topgallant sail, on the fore- and mainmasts. Until this time, however, the topmasts had been fixed extensions of the masts themselves and could not be rigged down. But around the 1570s, topmasts began to be stepped, to be fidded as the term was, so they could be rigged up or taken down depending on circumstances. This innovation, credited to the Dutch, was found to be very practical and was soon adopted for general use. Consequently, the fidded topmasts grew larger in relation to the lower masts; the topsail grew deeper, and the lower sail shallower.

Around 1620, it was common to equip the third mast with a square topsail. At the same time, the bonaventure mizzenmast was discarded. This marked the creation of the three-masted ship, with square sails on each mast. These early ships always had one yard less on the mizzenmast than on the fore- and mainmasts.

It was not until the latter half of the 18th century that rigging had evolved to the point where each mast had the same number of yards. This was the time when the term full-rigged ship became universal. The full-rigged ship usually referred to a merchant vessel, while sailing warships with such a rig were referred to by their rating: ship of the line, frigate, or sloop. The ships of the early 17th century were built with low heads and high sterns.

This design made them very hard to steer when the wind was abaft the beam, and the need for more headsail was keenly felt. To remedy the problem all larger ships of the 19th century were rigged with a spritsail topsail on a small mast at the end of the bowsprit. This sail was very impractical, though it was found to be very necessary, and it remained in use for over a hundred years before it was replaced with more practical and effective staysails.

Staysails had been used quite early in small craft, but not in the big ships. By the 1670s, however, the larger ships began carrying staysails, first between the masts and later over the bowsprit. This fore topmast staysail over the bowsprit was difficult to set because of the complicated rigging of the spritsail and sprit topsail. This was also the case with the staysails between the masts, because of the braces and bowlines leading to the stays. The staysails won out over the others, though, and in the beginning of the 18th century, the spritsail topmast was discarded and the running gear was gradually changed to make more room for the staysails of the mainmast. This development continued through the entire 18th century, and by the end of the century larger ships carried a staysail on every possible stay.

When the spritsail topmast was discarded in the first decade of the 18th century, a new spar, the jib boom, was rigged out on the bowsprit. A new staysail, called the jib, was placed over it ahead of the fore topmast staysail. After the middle of the same century, the lateen mizzen's long yard was exchanged for a gaff. This change occurred earlier in the smaller vessels than in the big ones.

During the Napoleonic wars, at the end of the century, other changes began to take place in the rigging. The mizzen was enlarged and sheeted to a boom extending over the stern. Under the bowsprit a new spar, called the martingale or dolphin striker, was inserted to improve the staying of the jib boom. This all developed into a new spar and staysail, the flying jib boom and flying jib, which were rigged outside the jib. A fourth yard above the topgallant yard, called the royal yard, now became more and more common on larger ships. Men-of-war always set it flying, while merchant ships set it as a standing sail carried on the upper part of the long topgallant mast. Only on hard winter trips was it rigged down. But this, of course, was true of all unnecessary rigging in prolonged bad weather.

The 19th century's mechanical revolution gradually began to influence the rigging of sailing ships. At first, it was merely a replacement on masts and yards of rope fittings, strops, and so on, with forged iron bands. Then the rope trusses of the lower yards were replaced with iron trusses, called patent trusses. Wherever possible, the heavier running rigging was replaced with chain, first the topsail ties and sheets and then the topgallant ties and sheets, and then just about anywhere chain

A

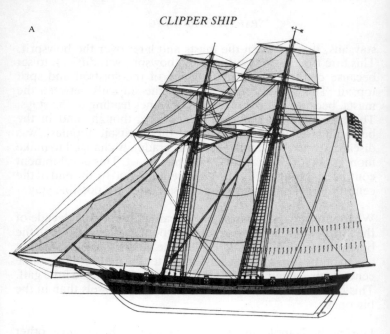

CLIPPER SHIPS

A The Baltimore clipper is considered to be the forerunner of the clipper ship. After the 1812 war with Britain, certain American shipbuilders built fast vessels, schooners and brigs, which could engage in the most profitable of the world's trades. Mainly built in Virginia and Maryland, these small beamy craft were known throughout the world as Baltimore clippers. Rigged as a two-topsail schooner and carrying a great spread of canvas, this example, from 1820, had a very raked stem and maximum draft aft. She mounted four small cannons on each side.

B FLYING CLOUD, 1851, build by Donald McKay at Boston, had single topsails, each with four reefs, topgallant sails with one reef, royals, and skysails. She had staysails on most stays and a whole set of studding sails, including the royals; she had studding-sail booms on the topgallant yards and jewel blocks for the royal studding sails on the royal yardarms.

C NORMAN COURT, 1869, a British tea clipper, had four headsails, double topsails, topgallant sails, royals and a main skysail. All sails are clewed up to the bunt; she has two reefs in the topsails and a standing spanker gaff.

B

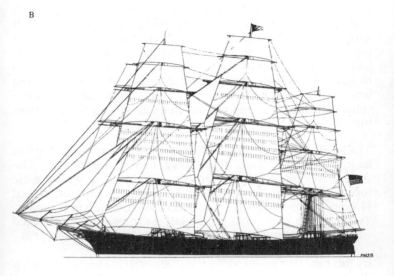

C

could be used to advantage. By the middle of the 19th century, British ships began to have the standing rigging replaced with wire. The rigging had previously been made of tarred hemp rope, but wire was cheaper and stronger and more durable. It had less surface exposed to the wind, and as the early attempts to build iron vessels were crowned with success, wire rigging was used more and more on larger ships, especially on steamships, which always had rigging and sails during the 19th century.

The huge topsails on larger sailing ships were extremely hard to handle during storms, when they had to be reefed. The American captain, Robert Forbes, devised a rig with double topsails in 1841. In 1854, another American sea captain, named Howes, improved this rig, and it became common in big ships. Twenty years later, in 1874, the largest ships were also rigged with double topgallant yards, as well as double topsail yards.

By this time, the use of wire for standing rigging and of chain for sheets and halliards was entirely accepted. Standing rigging now featured turnbuckles instead of deadeyes and lanyards, the system used ever since the early Middle Ages. Strong but stiff tarred hemp was replaced with Manila rope for running gear. Manila rope was softer and easier to work and just as strong, though not as durable as the hemp used formerly. Block sheaves were furnished with roller bearings, which also served to lighten the work on board ship. In fact, so much was done to ease the work on deck and aloft that the vessels could now be sailed with fewer hands, and larger ships could be sailed with the same crew as had been required for a smaller ship twenty years earlier. Sail handling became more mechanized in the large ships. In the 1890s, the Scottish sea captain, J.C.B. Jarvis, devised a geared mechanical winch that allowed a couple of men to brace the yards in the largest ships in rough weather. This was, of course, a big help. In the last of the big ships the topsail and topgallant halliards of chain were replaced with wire regulated by a hand-operated drum winch. Equipped with a conical drum, the winch considerably eased the effort of raising the yard.

All these innovations were part of that universal sequence of events that provided labor-saving devices in many areas of trade. For the sailing ship, these innovations had to be adapted to the special needs of the sea. They were needed to enable the sailing ship, with only the wind for power, to face up to the competition now provided by the coal- and oil-burning ships of the new age. It was obviously not a successful struggle, and the new means of propulsion became a prime factor in the disappearance of the sailing ship from all the seas of the world.

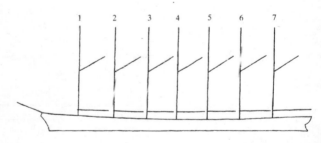

*Seven-masted fore-
and-aft schooner*
1 Foremast
2 Mainmast
3 Mizzenmast
4 Jiggermast
5 Driver mast
6 Pusher mast
7 Spanker mast

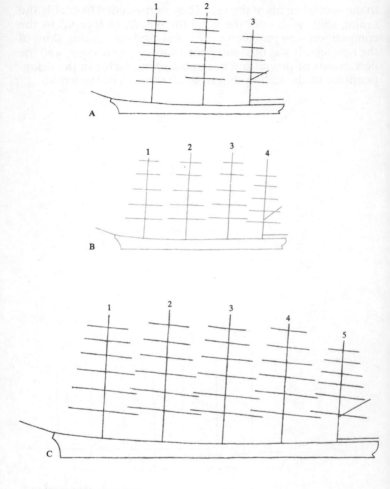

MASTS OF DIFFERENT SHIPS

A	*Three-masted fullrigged ship*	B	*Four-masted fulirigged ship*	C	*Five-masted fullrigged ship*
1	Foremast	1	Foremast	1	Foremast
2	Mainmast	2	Mainmast	2	Mainmast
3	Mizzenmast	3	Mizzenmast	3	Middlemast
		4	Jiggermast	4	Mizzenmast
				5	Jiggermast

MASTS

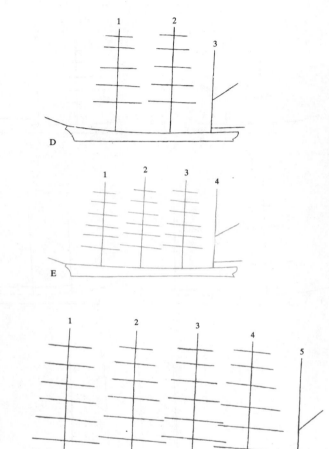

D *Three-masted bark*
1 Foremast
2 Mainmast
3 Mizzenmast

E *Four-masted bark*
1 Foremast
2 Mainmast
3 Mizzenmast
4 Jiggermast

F *Five-masted bark*
1 Foremast
2 Mainmast
3 Middlemast
4 Mizzenmast
5 Jiggermast

MASTS

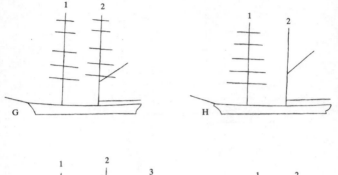

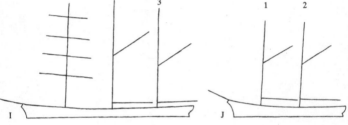

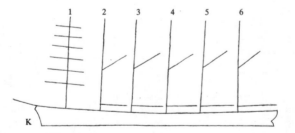

MASTS OF DIFFERENT SHIPS

G *Brig*	2 Mainmast	3 Mizzenmast
1 Foremast	3 Mizzenmast	4 Jiggermast
2 Mainmast		5 Driver mast
	J *Ketch*	6 Spanker mast
H *Brigantine*	1 Mainmast	
1 Foremast	2 Mizzenmast	L *Two-masted fore-*
2 Mainmast		*and- aft schooner*
	K *Six-masted*	1 Foremast
I *Three-masted*	*barkentine*	2 Mainmast
barkentine	1 Foremast	
1 Foremast	2 Mainmast	

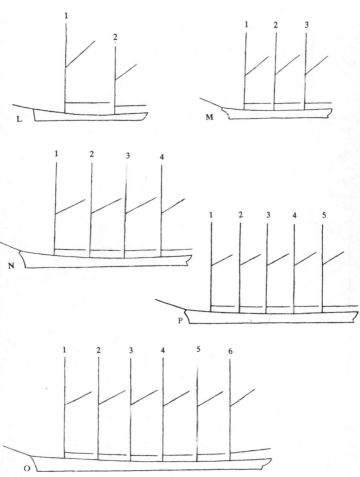

M *Three-masted fore-and-aft schooner*
1 Foremast
2 Mainmast
3 Mizzenmast

N *Four-masted fore-and-aft schooner*
1 Foremast
2 Mainmast
3 Mizzenmast
4 Spanker mast

O *Six-masted fore-and-aft schooner*
1 Foremast
2 Mainmast
3 Mizzenmast
4 Jiggermast
5 Driver mast
6 Spanker mast

P *Five-masted fore-and-aft schooner*
1 Foremast
2 Mainmast
3 Mizzenmast
4 Jiggermast
5 Spanker mast

89

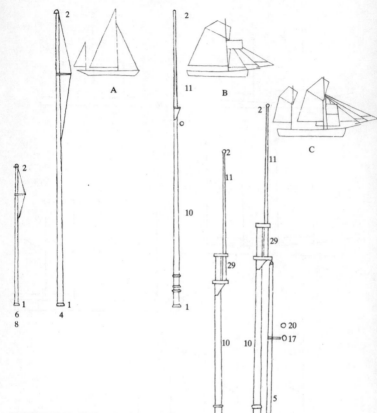

MASTS AND SPARS IN DIFFERENT SHIPS

A *Yawl*
B *Sloop, about
   1900*
C *Ketch, end of the
   19th century*
D *Topsail schooner*
E *Barkentine*
1 Mast coat
2 Truck
3 Foremast
4 Mainmast
5 Snow mast
8 Mizzenmast
9 Laeisz mast
10 Lower mast

11 Fore-and-aft-
   rigged topmast
12 Square-rigged
   topmast
13 Topgallant mast
14 Royal mast
15 Skysail mast
16 Moonsail mast
17 Fore yard
18 Main yard

19 Crossjack yard
20 Topsail yard for
   single topsail
21 Lower topsail
   yard
22 Upper topsail
   yard
23 Topgallant yard
   for single
   topgallant sail

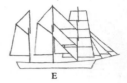

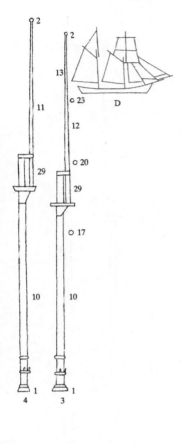

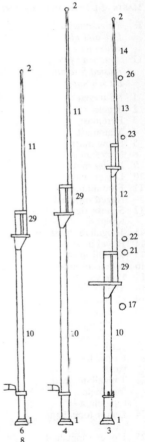

24 Lower topgallant yard
25 Upper topgallant yard
26 Royal yard
27 Skysail yard
28 Moonsail yard
29 Masthead and housing of top-mast

The terminology for masts varies in different languages. Numbers 5 and 7, missing in list above, refer to Teutonic languages only.

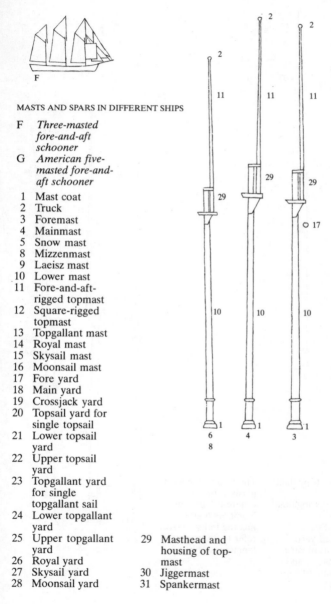

MASTS AND SPARS IN DIFFERENT SHIPS

F *Three-masted fore-and-aft schooner*
G *American five-masted fore-and-aft schooner*

1 Mast coat
2 Truck
3 Foremast
4 Mainmast
5 Snow mast
8 Mizzenmast
9 Laeisz mast
10 Lower mast
11 Fore-and-aft-rigged topmast
12 Square-rigged topmast
13 Topgallant mast
14 Royal mast
15 Skysail mast
16 Moonsail mast
17 Fore yard
18 Main yard
19 Crossjack yard
20 Topsail yard for single topsail
21 Lower topsail yard
22 Upper topsail yard
23 Topgallant yard for single topgallant sail
24 Lower topgallant yard
25 Upper topgallant yard
26 Royal yard
27 Skysail yard
28 Moonsail yard

29 Masthead and housing of top-mast
30 Jiggermast
31 Spankermast

G

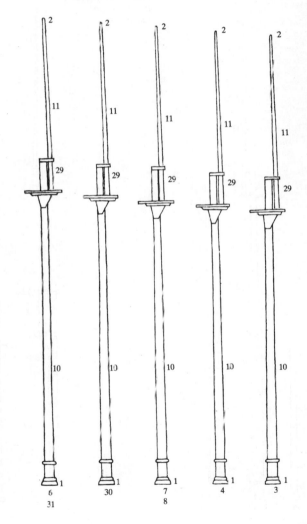

MASTS AND SPARS

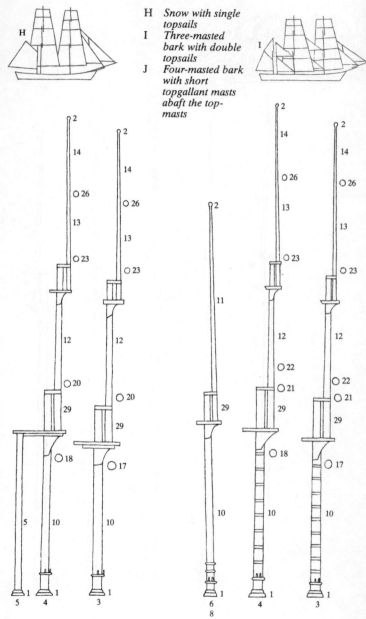

H Snow with single topsails
I Three-masted bark with double topsails
J Four-masted bark with short topgallant masts abaft the topmasts

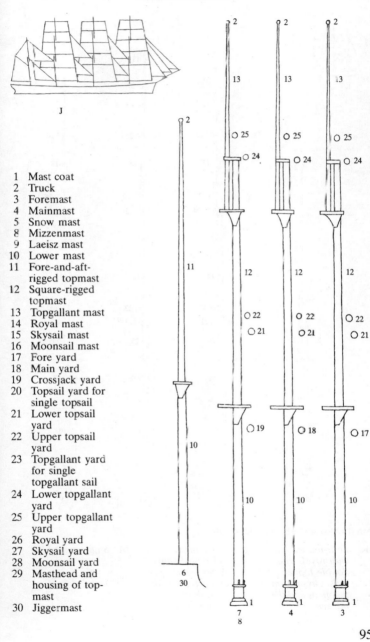

J

1 Mast coat
2 Truck
3 Foremast
4 Mainmast
5 Snow mast
8 Mizzenmast
9 Laeisz mast
10 Lower mast
11 Fore-and-aft-
   rigged topmast
12 Square-rigged
   topmast
13 Topgallant mast
14 Royal mast
15 Skysail mast
16 Moonsail mast
17 Fore yard
18 Main yard
19 Crossjack yard
20 Topsail yard for
   single topsail
21 Lower topsail
   yard
22 Upper topsail
   yard
23 Topgallant yard
   for single
   topgallant sail
24 Lower topgallant
   yard
25 Upper topgallant
   yard
26 Royal yard
27 Skysail yard
28 Moonsail yard
29 Masthead and
   housing of top-
   mast
30 Jiggermast

95

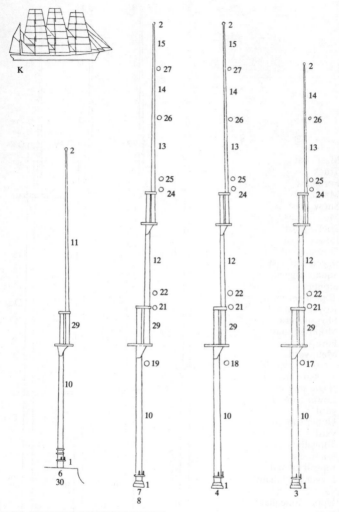

MASTS AND SPARS IN DIFFERENT SHIPS

K   *Four-masted bark with royals and double topgallant sails, skysails on the main and the mizzen*

L   *Three-masted, full-rigged ship, American clipper, about 1850, with skysails and a main moonsail*

M   *Ship, about 1700*

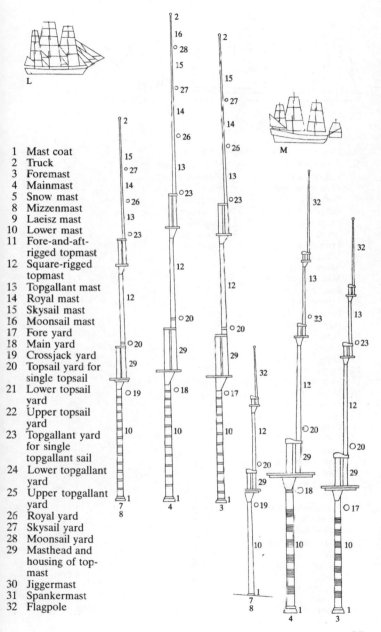

1 Mast coat
2 Truck
3 Foremast
4 Mainmast
5 Snow mast
8 Mizzenmast
9 Laeisz mast
10 Lower mast
11 Fore-and-aft-
   rigged topmast
12 Square-rigged
   topmast
13 Topgallant mast
14 Royal mast
15 Skysail mast
16 Moonsail mast
17 Fore yard
18 Main yard
19 Crossjack yard
20 Topsail yard for
   single topsail
21 Lower topsail
   yard
22 Upper topsail
   yard
23 Topgallant yard
   for single
   topgallant sail
24 Lower topgallant
   yard
25 Upper topgallant
   yard
26 Royal yard
27 Skysail yard
28 Moonsail yard
29 Masthead and
   housing of top-
   mast
30 Jiggermast
31 Spankermast
32 Flagpole

97

MASTS AND SPARS

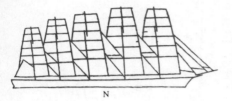

N

MASTS AND SPARS IN DIFFERENT SHIPS

N *Five-masted full-rigged ship (Preussen, the only ship of this rig ever built)*
1 Mast coat
2 Truck
3 Foremast
4 Mainmast
5 Snow mast
8 Mizzenmast
9 Laeisz mast
10 Lower mast
11 Fore-and-aft-rigged topmast
12 Square-rigged topmast
13 Topgallant mast
14 Royal mast
15 Skysail mast
16 Moonsail mast
17 Fore yard
18 Main yard
19 Crossjack yard
20 Topsail yard for single topsail
21 Lower topsail yard
22 Upper topsail yard
23 Topgallant yard for single topgallant sail
24 Lower topgallant yard
25 Upper topgallant yard
26 Royal yard
27 Skysail yard
28 Moonsail yard
29 Masthead and housing of topmast
30 Jiggermast
31 Spankermast
32 Flagpole
33 Laeisz yard
34 Jigger yard

98

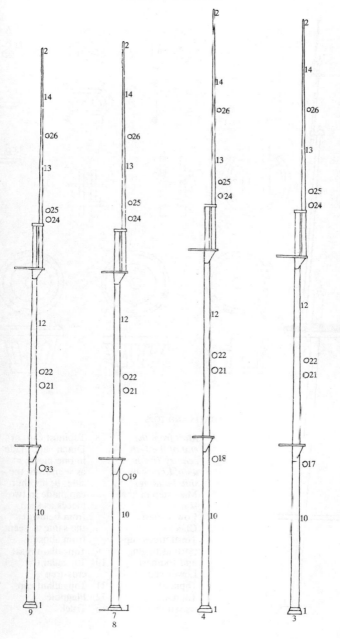

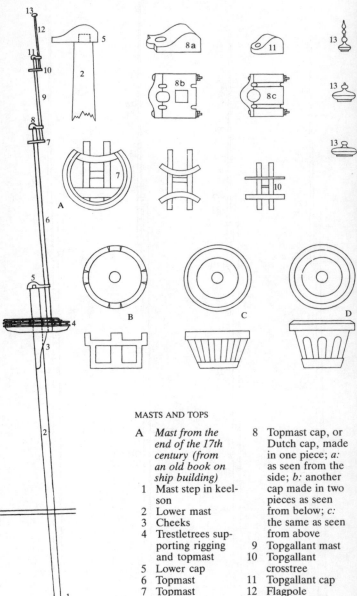

MASTS AND TOPS

A *Mast from the end of the 17th century (from an old book on ship building)*
1 Mast step in keelson
2 Lower mast
3 Cheeks
4 Trestletrees supporting rigging and topmast
5 Lower cap
6 Topmast
7 Topmast crosstree

8 Topmast cap, or Dutch cap, made in one piece; *a:* as seen from the side; *b:* another cap made in two pieces as seen from below; *c:* the same as seen from above
9 Topgallant mast
10 Topgallant crosstree
11 Topgallant cap
12 Flagpole
13 Truck

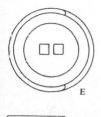

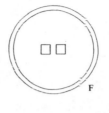

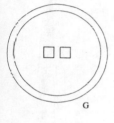

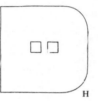

B   *Early medieval top*
C   *Medieval top*
D   *Medieval top*
E   *Top, about 1550*
F   *Top in the 17th century*
G   *Top in the 18th century*
H   *Top in the 19th century*

I   *Lower mast seen from port side*
1   Lower masthead
2   Trestletrees
3   Cheeks
4   Rope wooldings around the mast
5   Heel of mast

101

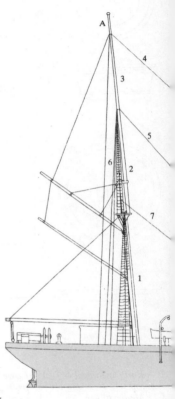

STANDING RIGGING OF A FOUR-MASTED BARK

A *Jigger mast* (identical with mizzenmast of a three-masted bark)
1 Jigger lower mast
2 Jigger topmast
3 Jigger topgallant mast
4 Jigger topgallant stay
5 Jigger topmast stay

6 Jigger topmast rigging or shrouds
7 Jigger stay
8 Jigger rigging or jigger shrouds
B *Foremast* (identical with mainmast and mizzenmast except in the lead of the stays)

1 Fore lower mast
2 Fore topmast
3 Fore topgallant mast
4 Fore royal mast
5 Fore royal stay
6 Fore topgallant stay
7 Outer jib stay
8 Inner jib stay
9 Fore topmast stay
10 Fore stay

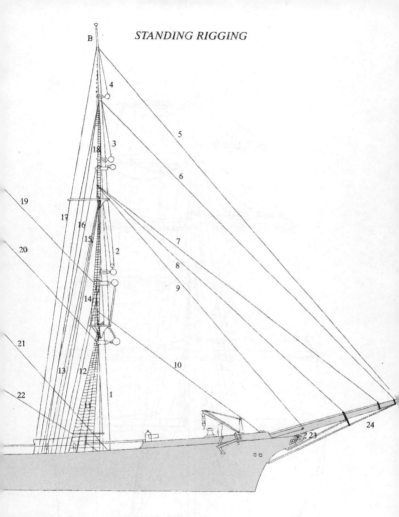

11 Fore rigging or shrouds	17 Fore royal backstay	24 Outer bob stay
12 Fore cap backstays	18 Fore topgallant rigging or shrouds	
13 Fore topmast backstays	19 Main royal stay	
14 Fore topmast rigging or shrouds	20 Main topgallant stay	
15 Fore topmast cap backstay	21 Main topmast stay	
16 Fore topgallant backstays	22 Main stay	
	23 Bob stay	

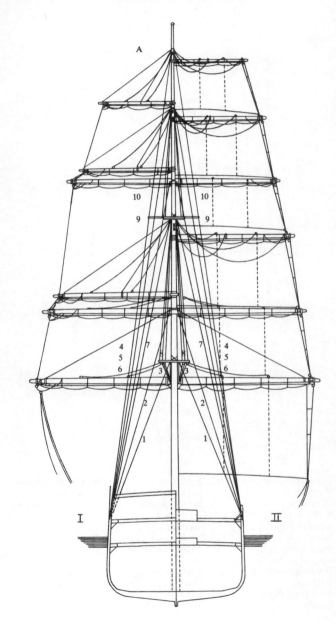

STAYS AND SHROUDS

A   *Square-rigged foremast of a big modern sailing ship as seen from aft, with the sails furled on the port side (I) and set on the starboard side (II)*
1   Lower rigging or shrouds
2   Cap backstay
3   Futtock rigging, futtock shrouds
4   Royal back stay
5   Topgallant backstay(s)
6   Topmast cap backstay
7   Topmast backstay(s)
8   Topmast rigging, topmast shrouds
9   Topmast futtock rigging
10 Topgallant rigging, topgallant shrouds
B   *This picture of a top, seen from the side, shows how shrouds and stays are fastened to the mast*

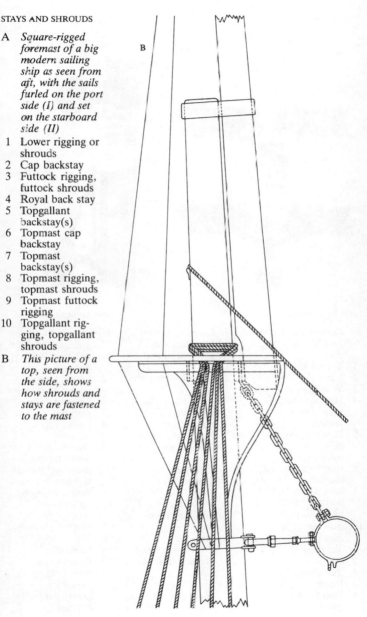

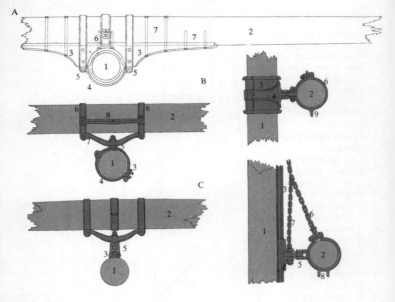

DIFFERENT PARRELS

A *Parrel with cleats
   on a wooden
   yard*
1 Topmast
2 Yard
3 Wooden cleats
4 Half-iron hoop
   served with
   leather
5 Pins forming
   hinges to open
   the parrel
6 Iron band to take
   the tie
7 Iron straps and
   bolts securing
   parrel to yard
B *Tub parrel for
   iron yard*
1 Topmast
2 Yard
3 Tub divided in
   halves
4 Iron binding for
   same

5 Gooseneck bolt
6 Iron bands to
   take parrel and
   tie
7 Yoke for the par-
   rel
8 Yoke for the tie
9 Eye bolt for
   quarterblock
C *Parrel, sliding on
   T-bar in a big
   ship*
1 Topmast
2 Topsail yard
3 T-bar
4 Slide
5 Two-way coup-
   ling
6 Tie
7 Connecting chain
   keeping slide in
   place
8 Eye bolts for
   quarterblocks

TOP AND CROSSTREES

Details around the top
1 Topmast, built in
   one with lower
   mast
2 Lower topsail
   yard with its truss
3 Lower topsail
   yard tie
4 Lower cap
   backstays
5 Quarter block for
   upper topsail
   sheet and topsail
   clewline
6 Topmast rigging,
   ratlines not
   shown
7 Futtock shrouds
8 Top
9 Fairleader
10 Running gear
   rove through
   fairleader
11 Lower yard with
   its truss

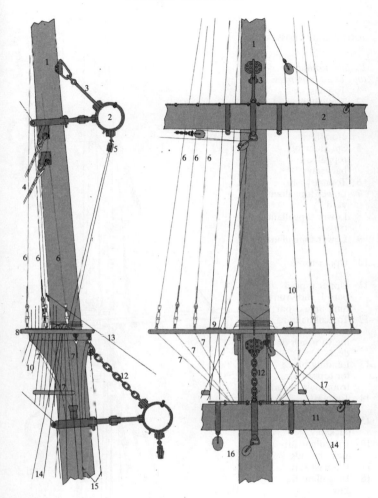

12 Lower yard tie
13 Lower stay,
    doubled
14 Lower rigging,
    ratlines not
    shown
15 Pendants for
    braces from mast
    ahead, leading to
    brace winch
16 Quarterblock for
    topsail sheet and
    the course
    clewgarnet
17 Buntline with its
    leading blocks

107

TOPGALLANT CROSSTREES

Details around the topgallant crosstrees

1 Topmast
2 Topgallant mast
3 Topmast head
4 Topgallant crosstrees
5 Spreader of topgallant backstays
6 Topmast cap
7 Lower topgallant yard
8 Lower topgallant truss
9 Lower topgallant tie
10 Upper topsail yard
11 Upper topsail parrel, slide running on a T-bar
12 Topsail halliard, wire tackle leading to winch on deck
13 Leading block for topsail brace from mast ahead
14 Topmast backstays
15 Topmast cap backstay
16 Topgallant futtock shrouds
17 Topmast stay
18 Topgallant rigging
19 Spreader lift
20 Quarterblock for lower topgallant clewline and upper topgallant sheet
21 Quarterblock for topsail downhaul and lower topgallant sheet

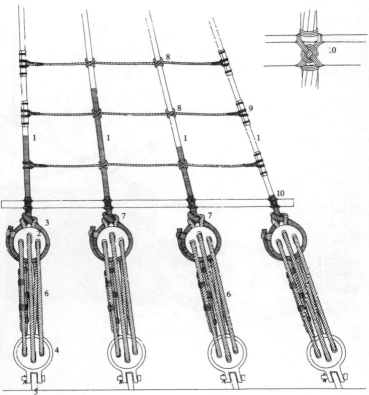

LOWER PART OF RIGGING, PORT SIDE

1 Shrouds, lower
   ends of which are
   served with spun
   yarn
2 Upper deadeye
3 Deadeye turned
   in cutter-stay
   fashion
4 Lowerdeadeye in
   iron strap
5 Chain plate
6 Lanyard, stand-
   ing part with wall
   knot
7 Hauling end of
   lanyard hitched
8 Ratlines in rig-
   ging
9 Seizing of ratline
   to shroud
10 Wooden batten
   secured to shroud
   with seizing wire

109

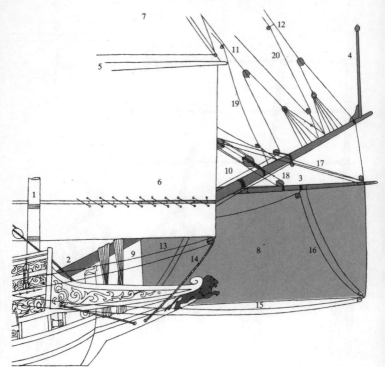

BOWSPRITS

The bowsprit and its rigging at the end of the 16th century

1 Foremast
2 Bowsprit
3 Spritsail yard
4 Jackstaff
5 Foreyard
6 Foresail with bonnet
7 Fore topsail
8 Spritsail
9 Gammoning
10 Forestay lanyard
11 Fore topmast stay
12 Fore topgallant stay
13 Fore sheet
14 Fore tack
15 Spritsail sheet
16 Spritsail clewline
17 Spritsail braces
18 Spritsail lifts
19 Fore topsail bowline
20 Fore topgallant bowline

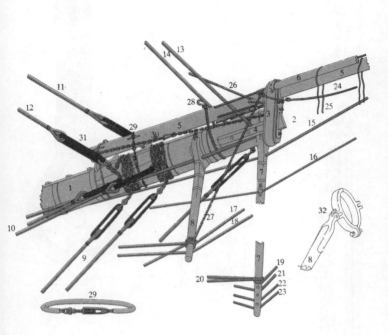

BOWSPRIT OF A FRIGATE, 1890

1 Bowsprit	13 Fore topmast stay	25 Gaskets
2 Tenon for bowsprit cap	14 Fore topmast preventer stay	26 Fore topsail bowline
3 Bowsprit cap	15 Jib stay	27 Whisker lift
4 Bowsprit bees	16 Jib outhaul	28 Fore topmast staysail tack
5 Jib boom	17 Jib boom guy	29 Jib boom gammoning
6 Heel of flying jib boom	18 Flying jib boom guy	30 Jib boom heel stay
7 Martingale boom or dolphin striker	19 Martingale stay	31 Lanyards for stays
8 Whisker	20 Backropes or martingale guys	32 Iron fitting for whiskers
9 Inner and outer bobstays	21 Flying jib stay	
10 Bowsprit shrouds	22 Fore topgallant stay	
11 Forestay	23 Fore royal stay	
12 Preventer forestay	24 Jib boom horse, footrope	

111

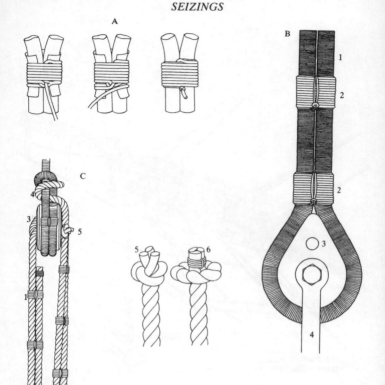

SEIZINGS AND RIGGING SCREWS

A *Three stages of making an old-fashioned round seizing; formerly used on hemp shrouds*

B 1 Shroud or backstay of wire served over with spun yarn
  2 Rigging seizings of galvanized wire
  3 Solid heart thimble with a hole for the sheer pole
  4 Upper end of rigging screw

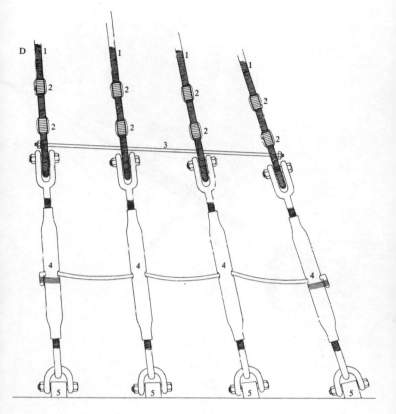

C *Details from lower part of rigging, port side.*
1 Surplus end of lanyard, made up
2 Lower deadeye in iron strap
3 Upper deadeye
4 Hauling end of lanyard, hitched
5 Wall knot
6 Double wall knot

D 1 Lower ends of four port side shrouds
2 Rigging seizings
3 Sheer Pole
4 Rigging screws or turnbuckles
5 Upper ends of chain plates

113

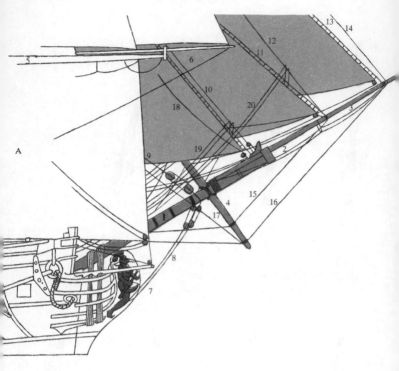

BOWSPRIT

A	*Bowsprit with jib boom and rigging, end of the 18th century*	11	Jibstay
		12	Fore topgallant stay
1	Bowsprit	13	Flying jibstay
2	Jib boom	14	Royal stay
3	Flying jib boom	15	Jib boom guy
4	Spritsail yard	16	Flying jib boom guy
5	Foreyard	17	Spritsail braces
6	Studdingsail boom	18	Fore topmast staysail downhaul
7	Fore tack bumpkin	19	Weather side jib sheet
8	Bobstay	20	Weather side flying jib sheet
9	Forestay		
10	Fore topmast stay		

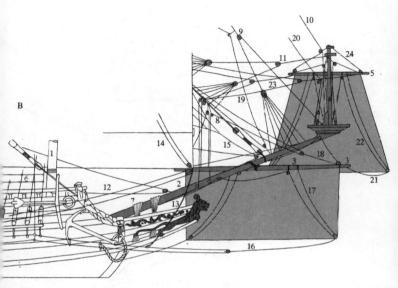

B   *Bowsprit with
     spritsail topmast
     and rigging, from
     the 17th century*
1   Foremast
2   Bowsprit
3   Spritsail yard
4   Spritsail topmast
5   Spritsail topsail
     yard
6   Fore rigging
7   Gammoning
8   Forestay
9   Fore topmast stay
10   Fore topgallant
     stay

11   Spritsail topmast
     backstay
12   Fore sheet
13   Fore tack
14   Fore clewgarnet
15   Fore bowline
16   Spritsail sheet
17   Spritsail clewline
18   Spritsail braces
19   Fore topsail
     bowline
20   Fore topgallant
     bowline
21   Spritsail topsail
     sheet

22   Spritsail topsail
     clewline
23   Spritsail topsail
     braces
24   Spritsail topsail
     lift

115

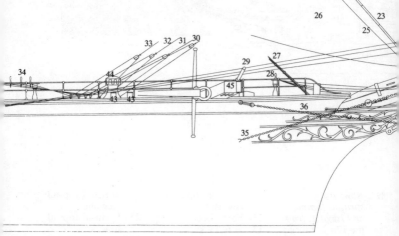

BOWSPRIT OF THE SHIP, PRINCE OSCAR, BUILT IN 1864

1	Shark's tail	8	Outer jib stay
2	Fore royal stay	9	Outer jib tack
3	Fore topgallant stay	10	Outer jib downhaul
4	Flying jib tack	11	Outer jib
5	Flying jib downhaul	12	Inner jib stay
6	Flying jib	13	Inner jib tack
7	Flying jib boom	14	Inner jib downhaul

15	Inner jib
16	Flying jib boom guy
17	Outer jib boom guy
18	Inner jib boom guy
19	Bowsprit cap
20	Swinging boom,

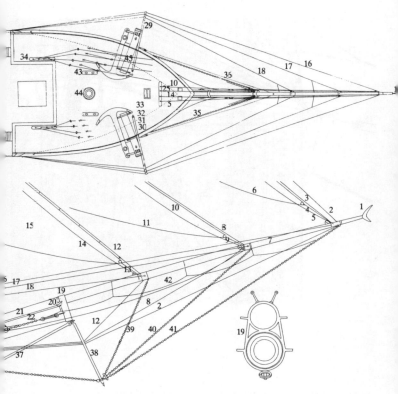

	fore guy lead		downhauls		Dolphin striker
	block	29	Whisker boom	39	Inner martingale
21	Jib boom	30	Flying jib sheet		(stay)
22	Bowsprit	31	Outer jib sheet	40	Middle mar-
23	Fore topmast stay	32	Inner jib sheet		tingale (stay)
24	Fore topmast	33	Fore topmast	41	Outer martingale
	staysail tack		staysail sheet		(stay)
25	Fore topmast	34	Pinrail	42	Foot rope
	staysail downhaul	35	Bowsprit shroud	43	Bitts
26	Fore topmast	36	Martingale	44	Capstan working
	staysail		backrope (Mar-		the windlass
27	Fore stay		tingale guy)	45	Cathead
28	Pinrail for	37	Bobstay		
	staysails'	38	Martingale or		

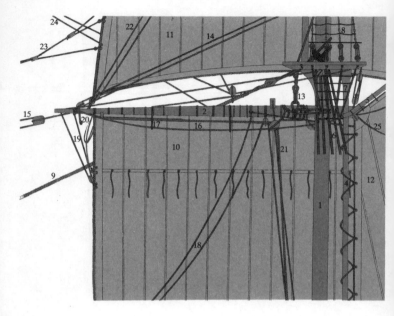

DETAILS OF MAINMAST AND MAINYARD OF A SNOW, ABOUT 1800

1	Mainmast	17	Mainyard stir-rups
2	Mainyard		
3	Main top	18	Main clewgarnet
4	Trysail mast	19	Reef tackle
5	Trysail gaff	20	Reef earing
6	Main rigging or shrouds	21	Topsail sheet
7	Futtock shrouds	22	Topsail clewline
8	Topmast shrouds	23	Topsail bowline bridle
9	Mainstay	24	Fore topsail brace
10	Mainsail	25	Trysail brails
11	Main topsail		
12	Trysail		
13	Mainyard sling		
14	Main lift		
15	Main brace		
16	Mainyard footrope		

DETAILS OF MAINMAST HEAD, SHIP OF THE LINE, 1750

1	Mainmast	17	Main footrope
2	Trestle trees	18	Main clewgarnet
3	Maintop	19	Main topsail sheet
4	Lower masthead	20	Main jeers
5	Heel of topmast		
6	Main cap		
7	Mainyard		
8	Main parrel		
9	Parrel tackle		
10	Main rigging or shrouds		
11	Mainstay		
12	Spring stay		
13	Futtock shrouds		
14	Topmast shrouds		
15	Mizzen topmast stay		
16	Main lift		

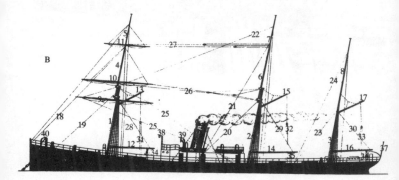

RIGGING OF OLDER STEAMERS

A, B
Steamer from about 1890, rigged as a three-masted topsail schooner

A   Fore topmast staysail
B   Fore staysail
C   Foresail; Boom foresail
D   Topsail
E   Topgallant sail
F   Main staysail
G   Mainsail
H   Main gaff topsail
I   Mizzen staysail
J   Mizzen
K   Mizzen gaff topsail

1   Foremast
2   Mainmast
3   Mizzenmast
4   Fore topmast
5   Fore topgallant mast
6   Main topmast
7   Main topgallant mast
8   Mizzen topmast

9   Fore yard
10   Topsail yard
11   Topgallant yard
12   Fore boom
13   Fore gaff
14   Main boom
15   Main gaff
16   Mizzen boom
17   Mizzen gaff
18   Fore topmast stay
19   Fore stay
20   Main stay
21   Main topmast stay

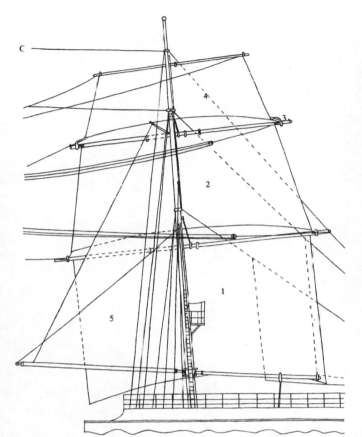

22	Main topgallant stay	32	Main vang		*the possibility of reefing without a man leaving the deck*
23	Mizzen stay	33	Mizzen vang		
24	Mizzen topmast stay	34	Boom foresail sheet		
25	Fore braces	35	Main sheet	1	Foresail
26	Topsail braces	36	Mizzen sheet	2	Topsail with Collin's and Pinkney's Patent (3)
27	Topgallant braces	37	Flagstaff		
28	Fore boom topping lift	38	Pole compass		
29	Main boom topping lift	39	Ventilator	4	Topgallant sail
30	Mizzen boom topping lift	40	Anchor davit	5	Bermuda-type trysail traveling on a bar abaft the mast
31	Fore vang	C	*Patent reefing topsails were not unusual in the old steamers carrying sails, because of*		

121

Opposite is a 1492 nao; it is Columbus' SANTA MARIA *and it introduces the section about sails. The color in the picture illustrates the fact that the chapter deals with flags as well.*

THE SAIL
By Sam Svensson

T he oldest sail we know is the square sail. For many thousands of years no other types were used. The distinguishing feature of the square sail is that the same side is always turned to the wind. This is a simple, fundamental principle, and none of the aerodynamic inventions of recent years have changed the square sail or influenced its value for sailing on the high seas.

The fore-and-aft sail, which can face into the wind with either side, is a more recent development. What aerodynamics could not do for the square sail it has succeeded in doing for the fore-and-aft sail. The latter is very effective in close-hauled sailing and is superior for use while cruising. Today, it is the sail most used for sport sailing among off-shore islands where winds are variable and the water is smooth. Because the fore-and-aft sail always has its forward bolt rope as the windward edge and the leech as the leeward edge, it can be cut with a favorable curvature. The square sail, on the other hand, has the starboard or port leech alternately as the windward edge, resulting in a different curvature. The value of the modern fore-and-aft sail on the wind is, however, outweighed by the advantages of the more secure square sail in running before the wind in stormy and high seas. Almost all sailing on the high seas has been done with the square sail. The oldest known reproduction of a boat equipped with a sail is painted on an Egyptian clay urn from the predynastic period. Estimated to be from about 4000 B.C., it could actually be even older. Furthermore, the evidence is not conclusive that this painting shows the world's first sail. Past cultures of which we have no knowledge may very well have had sailing vessels thousands of years before.

Contemporary writings and pictures prove that the sailors of ancient lands in the eastern Mediterranean used sails. In the twenty-seventh chapter of Ezekiel, the ships of Tyrus are described as having cedar masts from Lebanon, gay, embroidered sails of fine Egyptian linen, and awnings of blue and purple cloth from the Isles of Elisha. The decoration of the sails indicates that they were used both for propulsion and as a means of identification.

We have no record of when the art of sailing was brought to Scandinavia, but by the Viking Age it was certainly hundreds, perhaps even thousands, of years old. Early Nordic sails were made of homespun wool and lacked the durability of linen sails. The cloth would stretch under the force of the wind, and the large sail would sag more and more until it burst. To strengthen the sail and hold it more evenly, a supporting net was fastened to the forward side. The net, often of a different color than the sail, was either of rope, of cloth bands, or of interwoven sennit. The foot of the sail was held down by a number of sheets, forming bridles, all to hold the sail flatter. By the Viking Age, linen sails were in use on larger ships. These sails could be set flatter, making for better sailing on the wind. The long journeys made by the Vikings in European waters and over the Atlantic Ocean would have been impossible if their ships had not been able to sail in all kinds of wind. At the dawn of Swedish history, the cruising ability of the ships of the time is illustrated in the saga of the King of the Sveas, Erik Väderhatt, who, according to history, could turn the wind so that he never had a headwind.

The majority of ships continued to have only one mast and a single sail for many years. Only after the later Middle Ages did larger ships commonly appear with two or three masts and sails – one sail on each mast. By the end of the 15th century, however, a new sail was set at the head of the mainmast. It was originally very small and was handled by the men in the top (an early masthead castle). It derived its name, the topsail, from this position. Another sail was added under the bowsprit; this was called the spritsail or blind, as it blocked the view ahead. Eventually, a topsail was also added to the foremast. By the middle of the 16th century, then, a large three-masted ship carried six sails: the spritsail under the bowsprit, two sails on the foremast, two sails on the mainmast, and one sail on the mizzenmast. The sail on the mizzenmast was always a triangular lateen sail at this time.

The origin of the lateen sail is unknown. At the fall of the Roman Empire in 476 A.D., all ships had square sails. After that, sources of information on ships and navigation in the Mediterranean are not available for several hundreds of years. Not until the end of the 9th century do Greek manuscripts show some miniatures of ships with triangular sails under an inclined yard. Even today these sails are called lateen sails. These were probably introduced into the Mediterranean by the Arabs, but

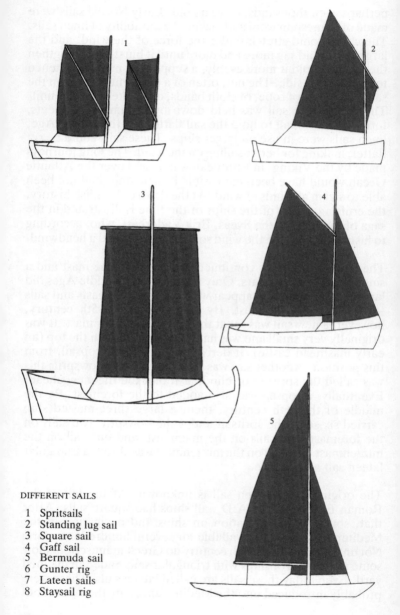

DIFFERENT SAILS

1 Spritsails
2 Standing lug sail
3 Square sail
4 Gaff sail
5 Bermuda sail
6 Gunter rig
7 Lateen sails
8 Staysail rig

126

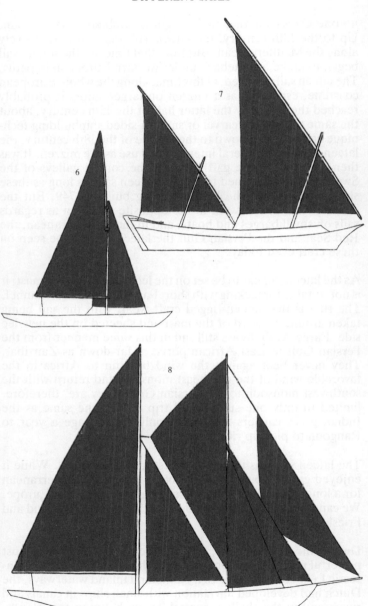

no one knows whether their origin is Arabian or Polynesian. Up to the 13th century, the lateen sail was in use exclusively along the Mediterranean. But from that time on, the square sail began to make a comeback under western European impetus. The lateen sail was used, at this time, along the whole European coastline, especially as a mizzen on larger ships. It probably reached the Baltic by the latter half of the 15th century, about the same time as the carvel or smooth-sided shipbuilding technique came along. Down to the middle of the 18th century, the lateen sail was in general international use as the mizzen. It was then replaced by the gaff mizzen. The coastal galleys of the Swedish navy continued to employ lateen sails as long as these ships were in use, the last one being built in 1749. But the development of sail went in the opposite direction as regards sails on small barges and boats, and in the Mediterranean, the Red Sea, and the Persian Gulf the lateen sail can be seen on these craft even today.

As the lateen sail has to be set on the leeward side of the mast, it is not suitable for tacking with short boards in a narrow channel. The rule is that lateen-rigged craft wear, with the sail being taken around forward of the mast and sheeted on the new lee side. Large Arab dhows still sail in this same manner from the Persian Gulf to East African ports, as far down as Zanzibar. They never beat against the wind but run to Africa in the favorable wind of the northeast monsoon and return with the southwest monsoon to the Persian Gulf. They are, therefore, limited to only one such round trip a year, the same as the Indian grain carriers that make only one voyage a year to Rangoon to pick up rice for Ceylon.

The lateen sail was the world's first fore-and-aft sail. While it enjoyed great popularity in the Near East and Mediterranean for a long time, other types of sail began to appear in Europe. We can follow this development especially well in Holland and Friesland.

During the 16th century, Holland became the world's most powerful maritime nation, replacing the sea power of the Hanseatic League. Using the rich Rhineland inland waterways, the Dutch had developed navigation with small ships in canals and rivers and in the shallow coastal waters between the islands.

The inability to beat and especially to tack in a narrow channel, when using a square sail, created the need for new types of sail, and Dutch art records two new fore-and-aft sails, the spritsail and the staysail. The former was a simple rectangular sail with one side laced to the mast and extended by a diagonally placed sprit. The sail was found to be very practical, and, as a result, it became the most commonly used sail in small sailing boats of Northern Europe. It was eventually used in larger craft as well and is now best known on the Thames River barges, which still use it today.

With the spritsail set abaft the mast, there was an empty space under the stay on the forward side of the mast, and it was only natural to set a triangular sail on that stay. By the middle of the first half of the 16th century, boats with a spritsail and fore staysail were in use in Holland. The development of the fore staysail was followed by a new staysail called the jib, which was set on a jib boom outside the stem. These staysails were soon in general use in small vessels in Western Europe, but it was not until the end of the 17th century that staysails appeared on the larger, square-sailed ships.

Another fore-and-aft sail, the lug sail, came to Europe somewhat later. The lug sail was a rectangular one that was hoisted with an inclined yard, with the halliard nearer the forward yardarm. Again there is evidence that the lug sail was known in the eastern Mediterranean about 100 A.D.

We are not sure whether the lug sail evolved from the lateen sail by cutting away the forward section or whether it came from the square sail by moving the halliard nearer one end of the yard and at the same time shifting the sail's tack amidships. The lug sail was used mostly in Western Europe, in the English and French waters of the English Channel. French fishermen and smugglers, as well as privateers and customs boats with sharp lines and fast hulls, were often rigged with lug sails; the type was sometimes called the *Chasse Marée*. English and Scottish fishermen in the North Sea also employed the lug sail, until they gave up the use of sails. Sailing ship's boats, both in the merchant marine and the navy, generally had lug sails as well, most often in one-masted, but also in two- or three-masted, rigs.

SAILS OF A FOUR-MASTED BARK

(HERZOGIN CECILIE)
This four-masted bark was built in 1902 by Rickmers shipyard at Bremerhaven for the Norddeutscher Lloyd at Bremen. It was a big sailing vessel of 3,242 gross tons or 4,350 dw. She was a good sailer and made many excellent voyages. During World War I, she was interned at Coquimbo, Chile.

After the war, she brought a cargo of nitrate to Ostend and was there allocated to the French government. In November, 1921, she was purchased by Gustaf Erikson, Mariehamn, and under his flag was employed chiefly in the Australian grain trade. She foundered on April 25, 1936, off Salcombe, Devon-

shire, after running aground in heavy fog.

1 Flying jib
2 Outer jib
3 Inner jib
4 Fore topmast staysail
5 Fore sail, fore course
6 Fore lower topsail
7 Fore upper topsail
8 Fore lower topgallant sail

9 Fore upper topgallant sail
10 Fore royal
11 Main topmast staysail
12 Main topgallant staysail
13 Main royal staysail
14 Main sail, main course
15 Main lower topsail
16 Main upper topsail

17 Main lower topgallant sail
18 Main upper topgallant sail
19 Main royal
20 Mizzen topmast staysail
21 Mizzen topgallant staysail
22 Mizzen royal staysail sail
23 Crossjack, mizzen course
24 Mizzen lower topsail

25 Mizzen upper topsail
26 Mizzen lower topgallant sail
27 Mizzen upper topgallant sail
28 Mizzen royal
29 Jigger staysail
30 Jigger topmast staysail
31 Jigger topgallant staysail
32 Lower spanker
33 Upper spanker
34 Gaff topsail

There were two types of lug sails: the standing and the dipping. The tack of the dipping lug was made fast a little before the mast, near the stem. It was always set to the lee of the mast and had to be shifted to the new leeward side at every tack. A standing lug had the tack at the mast and could take the wind from either side, though it was most effective when the yard was on the lee side of the mast. In ancient times, it was very common for the masts of fishing boats to have no shrouds, and one sailed only "on the wood," as it was called. The sail was set on the lee side of the mast, with the halliards leading to the weather quarter and serving as a backstay to sail on. Coming about, the sail was shifted to the new lee and the halliard to the new weather side.

In addition to the fore-and-aft sail on fishing boats and smaller vessels, the lateen sail in the Mediterranean, the lug sail in Western Europe, and the spritsail in Northern Europe, there were many small craft that still used square sails. The "Roslagen" sloops from Stockholm's archipelago used square sails until the end of the 18th century, as did the Norwegian "Nordland" yachts for as long as they used sails.

The original square sail, which had served maritime navigation for several thousands of years, was entirely different from the various kinds of fore-and-aft sails. When ships became larger and masts taller, the number of sails on each mast also increased. After the middle of the 16th century, the larger ships set a third sail, the topgallant sail, which was rigged above the topsail. In the beginning of the 16th century the larger ships set a third sail, the topgallant sail, which was rigged above the topsail. An impractical square sail, its mast was very badly stayed and often prone to damage. It remained in use on larger ships, however, for more than a hundred years, before it was replaced by a more practical staysail, the jib.

The first staysails on larger ships were set between the masts as the main staysail, the main topmast staysail, and the mizzen staysail. In addition, there was the fore topmast staysail, which was placed on a special stay from the fore topmast head and parallel with the fore topmast stay. This stay was actually so cluttered with blocks and running gear for the spritsail that the additional rigging for the new staysail caused many difficulties.

The fore topmast staysail was, however, a more effective head-sail than either of the square sails on the bowsprit, and at the beginning of the 18th century, the spritsail topsail disappeared. It was replaced, as was said earlier, by a new staysail called the jib. This was set on a new spar, the jib boom, which was rigged on the extension of the bowsprit.

By the beginning of the 18th century, rigging became more functional. The sails could be reefed effectively, and the rigging allowed for better bracing, which meant better sailing to wind-ward. The studding sail, which on occasion was already used in the previous century, became more common. It was used, when running free, to increase the sail area, much as the modern spinnaker functions on sailing yachts.

Toward the end of the 18th century, larger ships began to use a fourth square sail above the topgallant sail. It was called the royal. In men-of-war it was always set flying, *i.e.*, it was set from the deck, and when furled, it was taken down on deck. But in merchant ships it became a standing sail with the royal yard left aloft.

An important improvement in types of sail was made at the beginning of the 19th century, as the jackstay on the yards came into use. The head of the sail was bent to the jackstay on the forward upper side of the yard instead of having lashings around the yard. This made the work easier when bending and unbend-ing sail, and especially when furling sail. The sail could then be rolled up on top of the yards, where it could be easily secured under the gaskets. Without the jackstay on the yards, the larger steel ships of a later period could not have sailed with the small crews they had.

After the Napoleonic era, larger ships were rigged with a fifth sail, the skysail, which was carried over the royal. It was never widely used but was seen mostly at the time of the clipper ships, in the middle of the century. Some clippers carried still another sail, the moonsail, usually set only on the mainmast. Exaggera-tions could always be found, and one of the most unusual occurs in a story of the English corvette hunting for slavers in the steaming heat and calm waters of the Bay of Benin. Seamen tell of it carrying a royal, skysail, moonsail, heaven poker, angel poker, and cloud disturber — all over the topgallant sail.

133

A

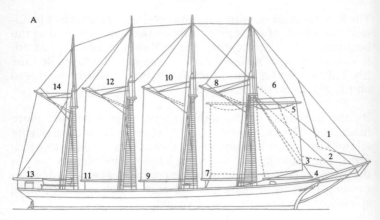

B

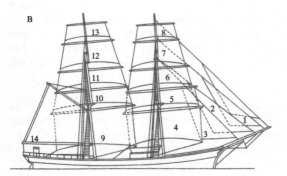

SAILS IN VARIOUS SAILING VESSELS

A	*Four-masted fore-and-aft schooner*	12	Mizzen gaff topsail	B	*Brig*
1	Flying jib	13	Jigger or spanker	1	Flying jib
2	Outer jib	14	Jigger gaff topsail	2	Jib
3	Inner jib			3	Fore topmast staysail
4	Fore staysail			4	Foresail
5	Square foresail			5	Fore lower topsail
6	Raffee			6	Fore upper topsail
7	Foresail			7	Fore topgallant sail
8	Fore gaff topsail			8	Fore royal
9	Mainsail				
10	Main gaff topsail				
11	Mizzen				

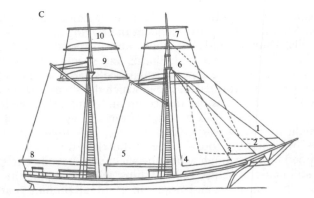

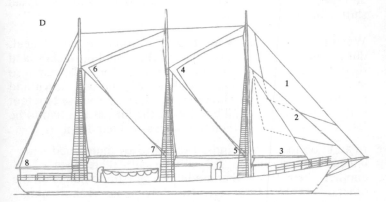

9	Mainsail	C	*Two-topsail schooner*	D	*Three-masted staysail schooner*
10	Main lower topsail	1	Flying jib	1	Flying jib
11	Main upper topsail	2	Outer jib	2	Jib
12	Main topgallant sail	3	Inner jib	3	Fore staysail
13	Main royal	4	Fore staysail	4	Fore trysail
14	Trysail	5	Foresail	5	Main staysail
		6	Fore topsail	6	Main trysail
		7	Fore topgallant sail	7	Mizzen staysail
		8	Mainsail	8	Jib-headed spanker
		9	Main topsail		
		10	Main topgallant sail		

Expanding 19th-century industry gave rigging a more delicate look. Mechanical improvements in the rigging also influenced the sails. Thimbles and clasp hooks were introduced, and, later, shackles. Both square-sail halliards and sheets were made of chain. Previously, the clews of square sails had been part of the bolt rope, which formed an eye in which the sheet and clewline were fastened. It now became common to put a thimble in the clew, and later to lead a cringle from the eye. Still later, a wrought-iron clew was spliced into the bolt ropes. In larger ships, with double topsail sheets, the clew was formed by a stropped block through which the sheet was reeved. The sheet was still made of hemp. In navy ships, where working the sails quickly became more and more important, all running gear was equipped with toggles, so that bowlines, buntlines, clewlines, and sheets could be let go in just a few seconds and a topsail shifted in just a few minutes.

When large ships began to be built of iron and then of steel, during the last half of the century, the standing rigging, and then the running gear, was made of wire. The sails were also influenced. The huge square sails were given both leech and foot ropes of wire, and a bolt rope of wire could be used for foot and leech on the staysail but not for the luff, as this had to be folded along the stay when the sail was hauled down.

In addition to the fore-and-aft sails already mentioned – the lateen sail, spritsail, staysail, and lug sail – there is yet another, the gaff sail, that gradually came to dominate all the others. It evolved from the spritsail by means of shortening the sprit, raising it, and fastening it to the sail's head. To keep it in place, with the forward end against the mast, the end was shaped as a throat or gaff with a branch fork, which partly covered the mast and gave both the spar and the sail its name, the gaff. To be able to hoist the gaff sail the mast had to be made higher than the sail, so that the gaff's halliards, the inner throat halliard, and the outer peak halliard could be fastened above the gaff.

Pictures of the gaff sail appear later than those of the spritsail but go as far back as the middle of the 17th century. Slowly, the gaff sail won out over the other fore-and-aft sails. Mail packets and other semi-official craft which sailed with mail and passengers between specified ports, revenue cutters, the larger pilot boats, and similar craft were among the first to use the gaff sail. During the 18th century, smaller merchant ships and war-ships began more often to be rigged with the gaff sail. Various types of early schooners and sloops all had gaff sails.

During the 19th century, larger merchant ships, for example the three-masted fore-and-aft schooners and barkentines, began to employ the gaff rig. Particularly in North America, by the end of the century, multi-masted fore-and-aft schooners began to show up. Many were four- or five-masted, several six-masted, and one was seven-masted. Some of them were extremely large sailing vessels that required steam winches to hoist their large gaff sails. They were at their best sailing on the wind in calm coastal waters; but they were difficult to run before the wind in hard weather. When they were used on deep-water voyages, their performance was usually much poorer than that of the square-riggers.

The gaff sail, however, soon became the most important sail for pleasure yachts. By the 17th century, the Dutch, English, and even the Swedes had gaff-rigged pleasure yachts. With the development of sport sailing and yacht clubs in the maritime nations, the gaff-rigged cutter became more and more popular, though it was sometimes surpassed in size by two- and three-masted, gaff-rigged pleasure schooners. At the beginning of the 20th century, the gaff sail was almost universally used in the yachting field.

Here, aerodynamic research performed a great service for sport sailing. As a result of new inventions, the wide gaff sail with a long boom is now almost as rare as the square sail. The only sail that has survived the extensive use of the motor yacht is the tall, narrow, gaffless boom sail, known as the Bermuda sail. Two hundred years ago, fishermen in Bermuda were using a triangu-lar mainsail without a gaff, but with a long boom. The modern yacht uses a sail which has only the name in common with that original Bermuda sail.

SAILS

SAILS IN VARIOUS SAILING VESSELS

A **Ketch**
1 Flying jib
2 Outer jib
3 Inner jib
4 Fore staysail
5 Mainsail
6 Main gaff topsail
7 Mizzen
8 Mizzen gaff topsail

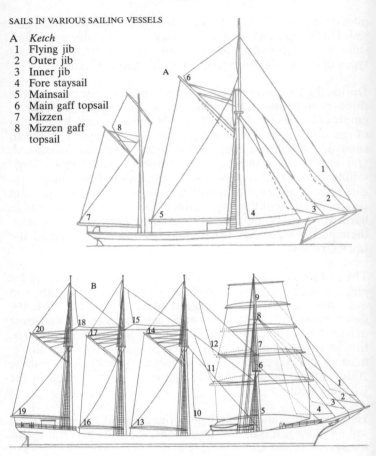

B	**Four-masted barkentine**		8	Fore lower topgallant sail	16	Mizzen
1	Flying jib		9	Fore upper topgallant sail	17	Mizzen gaff topsail
2	Outer jib		10	Main staysail	18	Jigger topmast staysail
3	Inner jib		11	Middle staysail	19	Jigger or spanker
4	Fore topmast staysail		12	Main topmast staysail	20	Jigger gaff topsail
5	Foresail		13	Mainsail		
6	Fore lower topsail		14	Main gaff topsail		
7	Fore upper topsail		15	Mizzen topmast staysail		

138

C *Sloop*
1 Jib topsail
2 Jib
3 Fore staysail
4 Square foresail
5 Mainsail
6 Gaff topsail

D *Full-rigged four-masted ship*
1 Flying jib
2 Outer jib
3 Inner jib
4 Fore topmast staysail
5 Foresail
6 Fore lower topsail
7 Fore upper topsail
8 Fore topgallant sail
9 Fore royal
10 Main royal staysail
11 Main topgallant staysail
12 Main topmast staysail

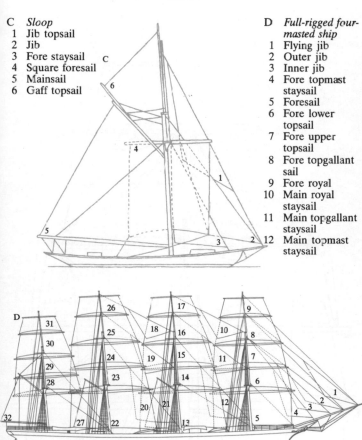

13 Mainsail
14 Main lower topsail
15 Main upper topsail
16 Main topgallant sail
17 Main royal
18 Mizzen royal staysail

19 Mizzen topgallant staysail
20 Mizzen topmast staysail
21 Main spencer
22 Crossjack
23 Mizzen lower topsail
24 Mizzen upper topsail

25 Mizzen topgallant sail
26 Mizzen royal
27 Mizzen spencer
28 Jigger lower topsail
29 Jigger upper topsail
30 Jigger topgallant sail
31 Jigger royal
32 Spanker

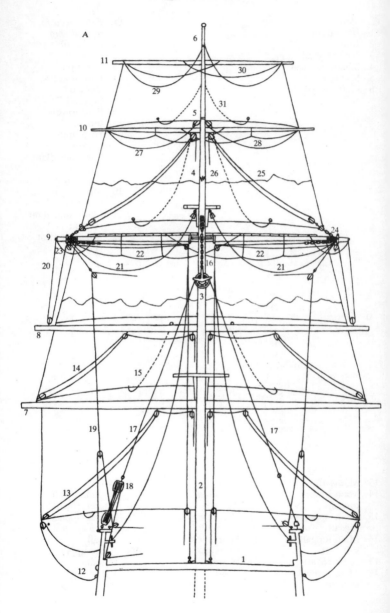

THE SQUARE SAIL

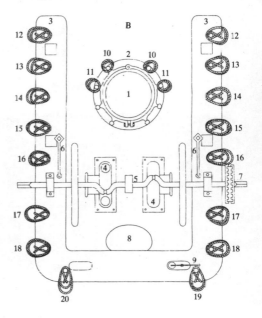

A *Square-rigged mast, seen from aft*
1 Deck
2 Lower mast with top
3 Topmast with crosstrees
4 Topgallant mast
5 Royal mast
6 Pole
7 Lower yard
8 Lower topsail yard
9 Upper topsail yard
10 Topgallant yard
11 Royal yard
12 Lower sheet
13 Clewgarnet
14 Topsail clewline
15 Lower topsail buntline, shown in broken lines forward of sail
16 Topsail halliard, tie
17 Topsail halliard, spanner
18 Topsail halliard, tackle or falls
19 Upper topsail brace
20 Topsail downhaul
21 Topsail lift
22 Upper topsail yard footrope
23 Upper topsail yardarm horse
24 Topgallant sheet
25 Topgallant clewline
26 Topgallant buntline
27 Topgallant lift
28 Topgallant yard footrope
29 Royal lift
30 Royal yard footrope
31 Royal buntline

B *Plan of fife rail at mizzenmast of a big sailing ship*
1 Section of mast with spider hoop
2 Mast coat at deck
3 U-shaped fife rail with belaying pins
4 Bilge pumps on deck
5 Pump axle with flywheels
6 Detachable pump cranks stowed on fife rail
7 Chain wheel for messenger from steam winch
8 Manhole from deck to pump well
9 Fresh water pump from tanks below deck
10 Lower topsail sheet
11 Upper topsail sheet
12 Crossjack clewgarnet
13 Inner crossjack buntlines
14 Outer crossjack buntlines
15 Crossjack lift
16 Mizzen topgallant sheet
17 Main lower topgallant brace
18 Main upper topgallant brace
19 Jigger topmast staysail downhaul
20 Jigger topgallant staysail downhaul

LOWER YARD AND SAIL

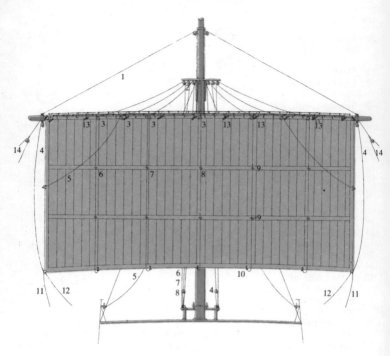

LOWER YARD AND SAIL, WITH RUNNING GEAR, IN A BIG SQUARE-RIGGED SHIP

1 Lift by which the yard can be trimmed either way out of the horizontal. In port, this can be done independently of the yards above and to a considerable angle. At sea, when sails are set, the movement is restricted, but affects all the yards on the mast.

2 Buntline blocks under rim of top
3 Buntline blocks on yard seized to jack stay
4 Clewgarnet by which the clews of the sail are hauled up to the yardarms
5 Leech line
6 Outer buntline
7 Inner buntline
8 Middle buntline
9 Bull's eye sewn to the sail to lead the buntlines

10 Buntline hitch
11 Tacks leading forward
12 Sheets leading aft; the clews of the sail are trimmed to the wind by tacks and sheets.
When the sail is to be furled, the tacks and sheets are let go and the sail is hauled up to the yard by the clewgarnets and buntlines.

142

YARD WITH DETAILS

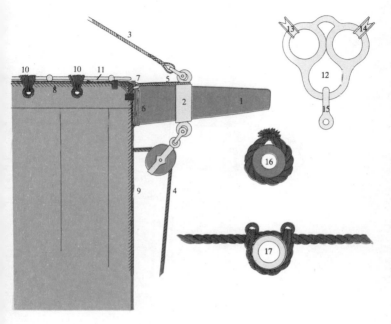

PORT SIDE YARDARM OF LOWER YARD, WITH DETAILS

Then men go
aloft, lie out on
the yard, and roll
up the sail tightly
and secure it by
tying the gaskets
around yard and
sail.

13 Gaskets
14 Braces leading
   aft, by which the
   yard is braced to
   different winds

1 Yardarm
2 Yardarm band
3 Lift shackled to
   yardarm band
4 Clewgarnet
5 Hauling out part
   of head earing
6 Round turns of
   head earing
7 Ring of head ear-
   ing
8 Head of sail
9 Leech of sail
10 Robands, tied
   with a square
   knot
11 Jack stay

12 Clew of
   galvanized iron
13 Thimble for foot
   of sail
14 Thimble for
   leech
15 Shackle for sheet
16 Bull's-eye sewed
   into sail
17 Cringle on bolt
   rope with round
   thimble

143

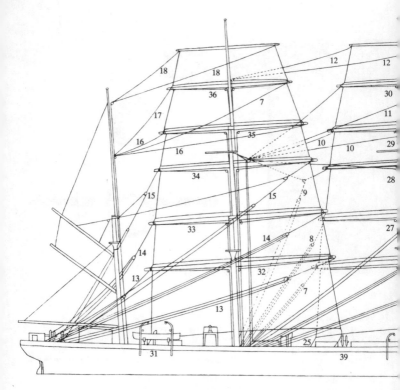

RUNNING RIGGING OF THE SQUARE SAILS OF A FOUR-MASTED BARK

Braces and sheets

1 Fore brace
2 Fore lower top-
   sail brace
3 Fore upper top-
   sail brace
4 Fore lower
   topgallant brace
5 Fore upper
   topgallant brace
6 Fore royal brace
7 Main brace

8 Main lower top-
   sail brace
9 Main upper top-
   sail brace
10 Main lower
    topgallant brace
11 Main upper
    topgallant brace
12 Main royal brace
13 Crossjack brace

14 Mizzen lower
    topsail brace
15 Mizzen upper
    topsail brace
16 Mizzen lower
    topgallant brace
17 Mizzen upper
    topgallant brace
18 Mizzen royal
    brace
19 Fore sheet

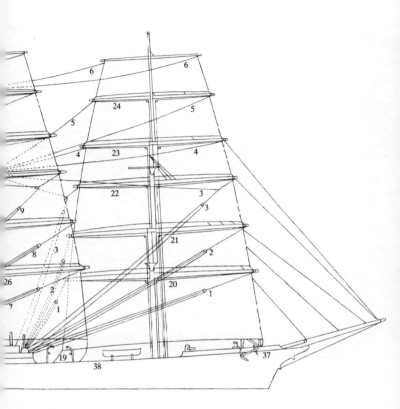

20	Fore lower top- sail sheet	sail sheet
21	Fore upper top- sail sheet	27 Main upper top- sail sheet
22	Fore lower topgallant sheet	28 Main lower topgallant sheet
23	Fore upper topgallant sheet	29 Main upper topgallant sheet
24	Fore royal sheet	30 Main royal sheet
25	Main sheet	31 Crossjack sheet
26	Main lower top-	32 Mizzen lower topsail sheet

33	Mizzen upper topsail sheet
34	Mizzen lower topgallant sheet
35	Mizzen upper topgallant sheet
36	Mizzen royal sheet
37	Fore tack
38	Main tack
39	Crossjack tack

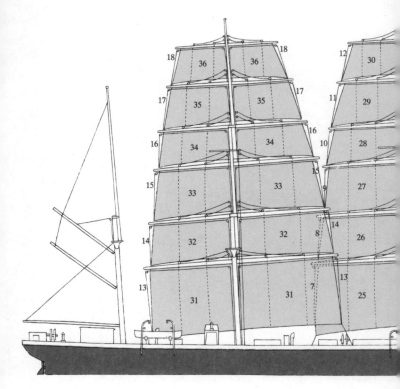

Buntlines, clewlines, and downhauls

1 Fore clewgarnet
2 Fore lower topsail clewline
3 Fore upper topsail downhaul
4 Fore lower topgallant clewline
5 Fore upper topgallant downhaul
6 Fore royal clewline

7 Main clewgarnet
8 Main lower topsail clewline
9 Main upper topsail downhaul
10 Main lower topgallant clewline
11 Main upper topgallant downhaul
12 Main royal clewline
13 Crossjack clewgarnet

14 Mizzen lower topsail clewline
15 Mizzen upper topsail downhaul
16 Mizzen lower topgallant clewline
17 Mizzen upper topgallant downhaul
18 Mizzen royal clewline
19 Fore buntlines
20 Fore lower topsail buntlines

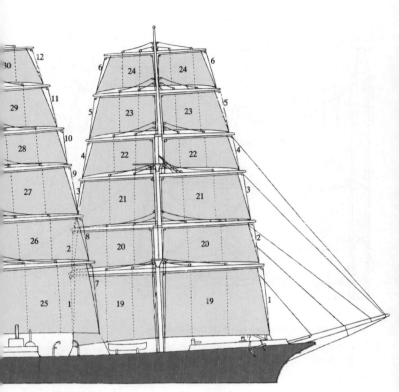

21 Fore upper top-
    sail buntlines
22 Fore lower
    topgallant
    buntlines
23 Fore upper
    topgallant
    buntlines
24 Fore royal
    buntlines
25 Main buntlines
26 Main lower top-
    sail buntlines
27 Main upper top-
    sail buntlines

28 Main lower
    topgallant
    buntlines
29 Main upper
    topgallant
    buntlines
30 Main royal
    buntlines
31 Crossjack
    buntlines
32 Mizzen lower
    topsail buntlines
33 Mizzen upper
    topsail buntlines

34 Mizzen lower
    topgallant
    buntlines
35 Mizzen upper
    topgallant
    buntlines
36 Mizzen royal
    buntlines

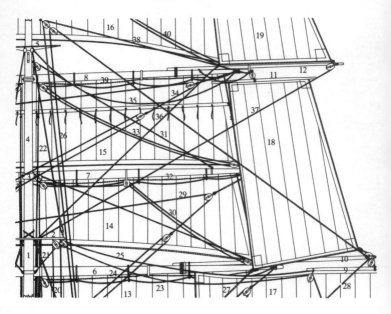

EARLY METHOD OF RIGGING DOUBLE TOPSAILS, 1860

1 Lower mast,
   foremast
2 Top
3 Cap
4 Topmast
5 Topmast
   crosstree
6 Lower foreyard
7 Lower topsail
   yard
8 Upper topsail
   yard
9 Lower studding
   sail yard
10 Topmast studding
   sail boom
11 Topmast studding
   sail yard
12 Topgallant stud-
   ding sail boom
13 Fore course,
   foresail
14 Lower topsail
15 Upper topsail

16 Topgallant sail
17 Lower studding
   sail
18 Topmast studding
   sail
19 Topgallant stud-
   ding sail
20 Lower rigging or
   shrouds
21 Futtock shrouds
22 Topmast rigging
   or shrouds
23 Lower yard
   footrope
24 Lower topsail
   sheet of chain
25 Inner lower stud-
   ding sail halliard
26 Outer lower stud-
   ding sail halliard
27 Topmast studding
   sail sheet
28 Topmast studding
   sail tack

29 Lower topsail
   brace
30 Lower topsail
   clewline
31 Lower topsail lift
32 Upper topsail
   sheet
33 Upper topsail
   clewline
34 Upper topsail
   brace
35 Upper topsail lift
36 Topgallant stud-
   ding sail sheet
37 Topgallant stud-
   ding sail tack
38 Topmast studding
   sail halliard
39 Topgallant sheet
40 Topgallant
   clewline

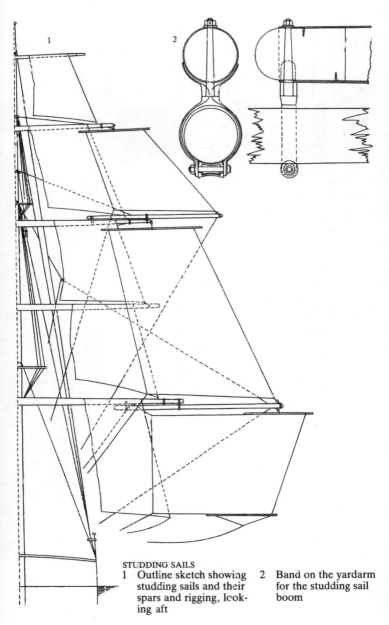

STUDDING SAILS
1 Outline sketch showing studding sails and their spars and rigging, looking aft

2 Band on the yardarm for the studding sail boom

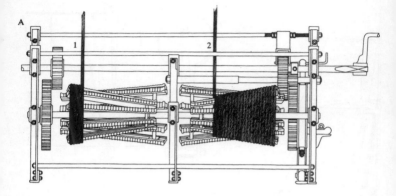

TOPSAIL HALLIARDS AND WINCHES

A *Brace winch invented by Captain J.C. Jarvis of Tayport, Scotland. The winch controls the lower brace and the two topsail braces, one winch for each mast. The winch has three axles, each with two barrels, and is so arranged with cogwheels that when the winch is turned, braces on one side pay out as those on the other side wind on.*
1 Weather side brace paid out
2 Lee side brace hove in

B *Topsail halliard of a barkentine*
1 End of chain span across the deck
2 Mousing on hook
3 Moving block, double

4 Becket, in one with the straps
5 Fall, two-fold purchase rove to advantage
6 Pin rail
7 Belaying pin
8 Main rail
C *Topsail halliard winch*
1 Flywheel with removable handle, which was removed after the sail was hoisted so as to be out of the way
2 Worm gear
3 Grooved barrel for the halliard, tapered to increase power as the yard ascends
4 Brake

5 Wheel with threaded shaft to control the brake. When the topsail yard was lowered, the brake was eased off and the flywheel was given a start with a push. This set the barrel revolving; the downward speed was regulated by the brake.

150

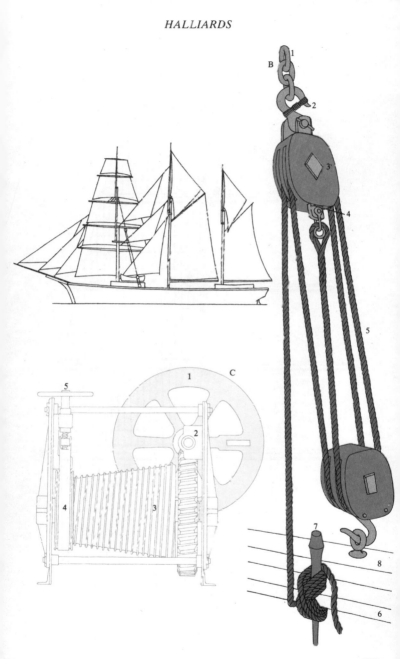

A

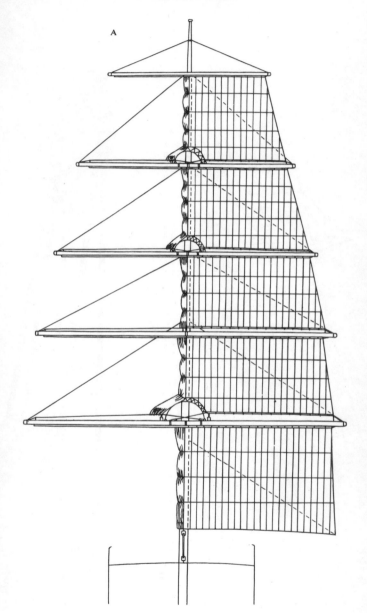

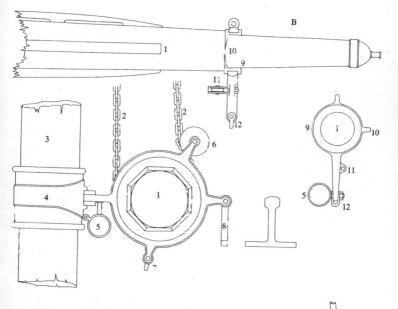

A *Square sail by the Rägener system* Many inventors have tried to improve upon the traditional square rig, which evolved empirically from centuries of experience gained the hard way. None did much to improve the old sailing ship, and this system by Rägener, with trussed yards and sails running on horizontal slides and brailed in to the mast, never got beyond the drawing board.

B *Cunningham's patent self-reefing topsail*
1 Revolving topsail yard
2 Bight of chain topsail tie
3 Topmast
4 Topsail yard parrel
5 Chafing spar to protect the sail when reefed
6 Roller lead for tie
7 Bolt for downhaul tackle
8 T-shaped bolt for the bonnet
9 Yardarm hoop within which the yard works
10 Bolt for topsail yard lifts
11 Leading block for topgallant sheet
12 Shackle to take the brace
13 Downhaul tackle
14 Twin runners of topsail halliards
15 Twin tackles of topsail halliards

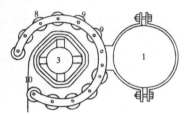

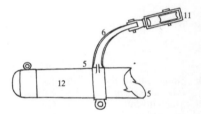

PATENT SELF-REEFING TOPSAIL

Colling's & Pinkney's patent self-reefing top-sail
1 Topsail yard
2 Parrel
3 Rolling spar
4 Iron drum end of rolling spar
5 Yardarm hoop
6 Arm carrying reefing halliard block
7 Cheek block for topgallant sheet
8 Parrel crutch with lignum vitae rollers
9 Lignum vitae rollers
10 Topsail
11 Lead block for reefing halliards
12 Topsail yardarm

SQUARE SAILS

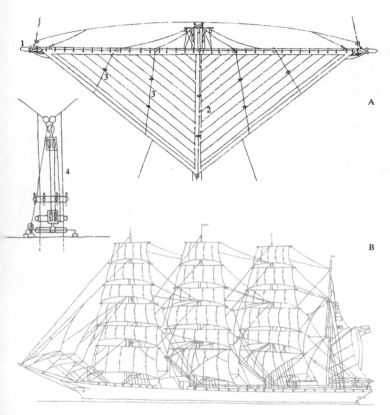

DIFFERENT RIGGING OF LOWER SQUARE SAILS

A *Big square-rigged sailing ships could, sometimes, set a three-cornered mainsail or cross-jack. Such a sail could be carried in a gale long after a square sail had to be taken in, but this advantage was counteracted by* *the fact that the three-cornered sail gave less spread of canvas in a moderate wind. The numbers indicate:*

1 Lower yard
2 Three-cornered sail
3 Buntlines
4 Tackle sheet in front of mast

B *A four-masted bark under all sail, setting a three-cornered crossjack, while the mainsail is drawn double showing both a square sail and a three-cornered sail*

155

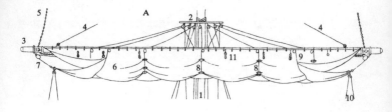

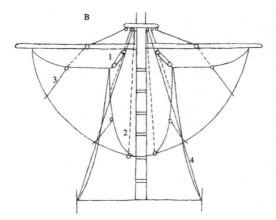

CLEWED MAINSAILS

A *A mainsail, clewed up to the yardarm, as seen from forward*
1 Lower mast
2 The top
3 Lower yard
4 Lifts
5 Lower topsail sheet, sail clewed up to the yardarm

6 The sail, say, mainsail
7 Clewgarnets
8 Buntlines
9 Leechlines
10 Tacks and sheets
11 Gaskets

B *A mainsail with the clews hauled up as seen from aft*
1 Clewgarnets
2 Buntlines
3 Leechlines
4 Sheets

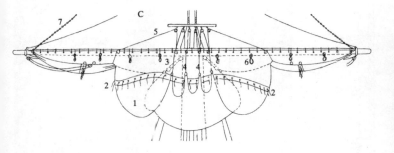

C

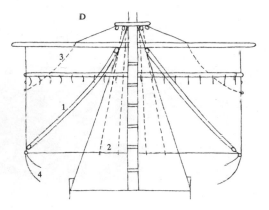

D

C *A mainsail*
  clewed up in the
  bunt as seen from
  forward
1 The sail
2 Reef band
3 Clewgarnets
  abaft the sail
4 Buntlines
5 Leechlines
6 Gaskets

7 Lower topsail
  sheet, sail clewed
  up in the bunt

D *A mainsail*
  clewed up in the
  bunt as seen from
  aft
1 Clewgarnets
2 Buntlines
3 Leechlines
4 Sheet

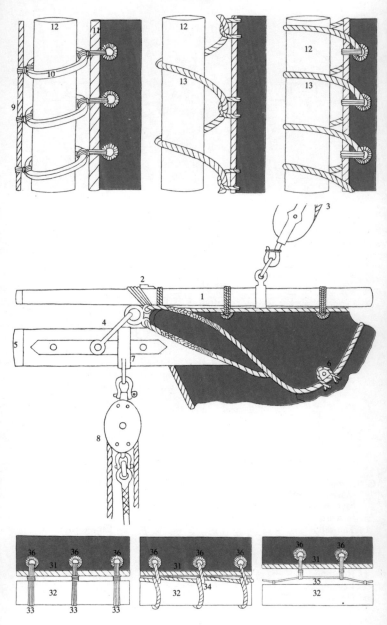

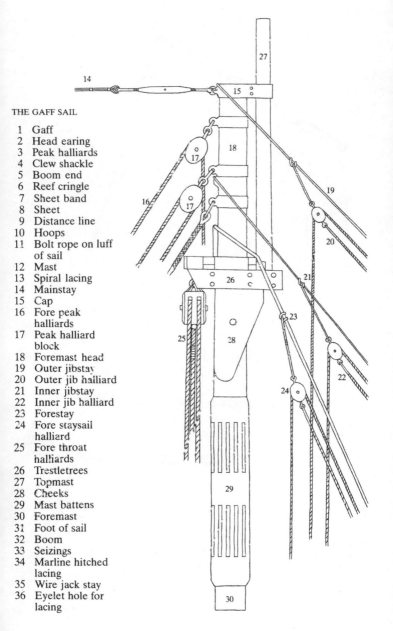

GAFF SAIL

THE GAFF SAIL

1 Gaff
2 Head earing
3 Peak halliards
4 Clew shackle
5 Boom end
6 Reef cringle
7 Sheet band
8 Sheet
9 Distance line
10 Hoops
11 Bolt rope on luff of sail
12 Mast
13 Spiral lacing
14 Mainstay
15 Cap
16 Fore peak halliards
17 Peak halliard block
18 Foremast head
19 Outer jibstay
20 Outer jib halliard
21 Inner jibstay
22 Inner jib halliard
23 Forestay
24 Fore staysail halliard
25 Fore throat halliards
26 Trestletrees
27 Topmast
28 Cheeks
29 Mast battens
30 Foremast
31 Foot of sail
32 Boom
33 Seizings
34 Marline hitched lacing
35 Wire jack stay
36 Eyelet hole for lacing

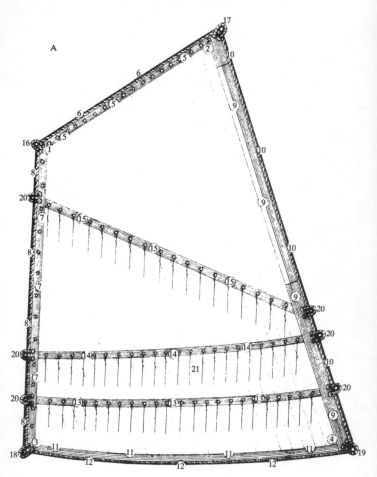

THE GAFF SAIL (FROM PAASCH)

A	*Gaff sail*	8	Luff rope	15	Balance reef
1	Throat	9	Leech		band
2	Peak	10	Leech rope	16	Throat cringle
3	Tack	11	Foot	17	Peak cringle
4	Clew	12	Foot rope	18	Tack cringle
5	Head	13	First reef band	19	Clew cringle
6	Headrope	14	Second reef band	20	Reef cringles
7	Luff			21	Reef points

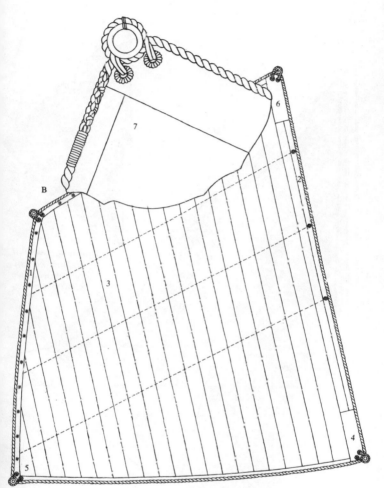

B *A spanker,
which sets under
a standing gaff
and brails in to
the mast (leeches
and cringles
made as in* A)

1 Half a cloth tab-
ling on the luff
2 Folding on the
after leech with
three holes to
take the brails
3 Lead of brails
across the sail

4 Sheet patch
5 Tack patch
6 Peak patch
7 Detail of peak
cringle

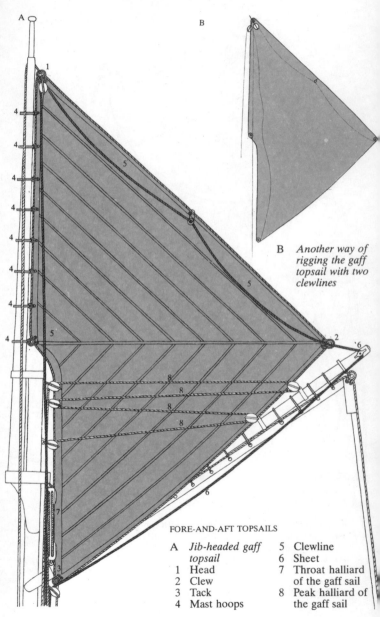

B *Another way of
rigging the gaff
topsail with two
clewlines*

FORE-AND-AFT TOPSAILS

A	*Jib-headed gaff topsail*	5	Clewline
1	Head	6	Sheet
2	Clew	7	Throat halliard of the gaff sail
3	Tack	8	Peak halliard of the gaff sail
4	Mast hoops		

162

GAFF TOPSAIL

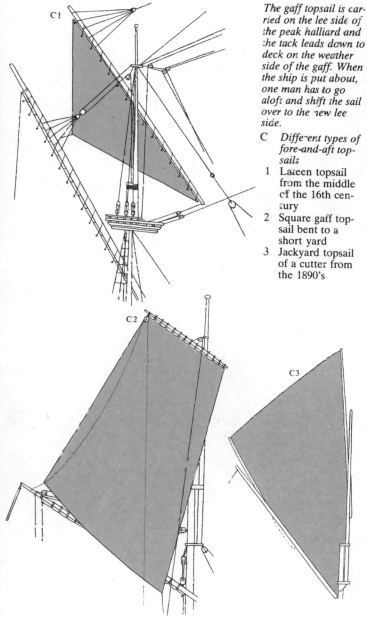

The gaff topsail is carried on the lee side of the peak halliard and the tack leads down to deck on the weather side of the gaff. When the ship is put about, one man has to go aloft and shift the sail over to the new lee side.

C Different types of fore-and-aft topsails

1 Lateen topsail from the middle of the 16th century

2 Square gaff topsail bent to a short yard

3 Jackyard topsail of a cutter from the 1890's

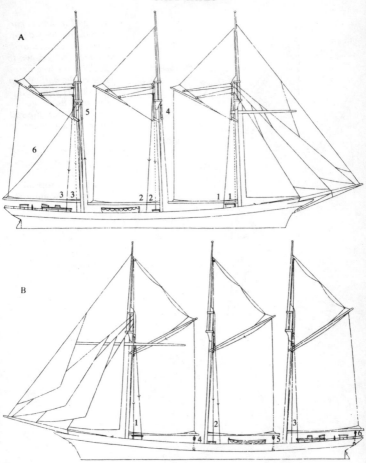

GAFF SAILS

A *The peak
   halliards and top-
   ping lifts of the
   gaff sails on
   board a three-
   masted fore-and-
   aft schooner*

1 Fore peak
   halliard
2 Main peak
   halliard

3 Mizzen peak
   halliard
4 Fore topping lift
5 Main topping lift
6 Mizzen topping
   lift

B *The throat
   halliards and
   sheets of the gaff
   sails on board a
   three-masted fore-
   and-aft schooner*

1 Fore throat
   halliard
2 Main throat
   halliard

C

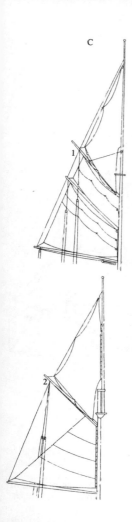

3 Mizzen throat
halliard
4 Fore sheet
5 Main sheet
6 Mizzen sheet or
spanker sheet

C *Different gaff
sails*
1 Upper and lower
spanker of the
five-masted bark
Potosi
2 Jigger of the
four-masted bark
Archibald Russell

3 Spanker of a big
American fore-
and-aft schooner.
The vertical
ropes (4) from
the topping lift
are called lazy
jacks.

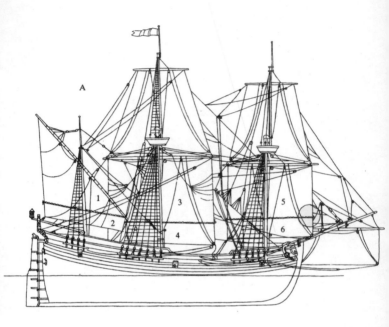

BONNETS AND REEFS

A   A merchant ship
    from the first half
    of the 17th cen-
    tury. Additional
    sails, called bon-
    nets, are laced to
    the foot of her
    courses and la-
    teen mizzen. Sail
    area can be
    reduced by unlac-
    ing the bonnets.
1   Mizzen
2   Mizzen bonnet
3   Mainsail
4   Main bonnet
5   Foresail
6   Fore bonnet

B   The bonnets were
    laced to the sails
    in such a way as
    to make the lac-
    ing spill itself
    once it was
    started; this made
    quick work of
    shortening sail
1   Lower sail
2   Bonnet
3   The clew of the
    sail seized to the
    earing of the
    bonnet
4   The leech rope of
    the bonnet, end-
    ing in a wall knot

and stropped to
the leech of the
sail
5   Lacing of head of
    bonnet to foot of
    sail is made to
    spill once its stop
    is let go

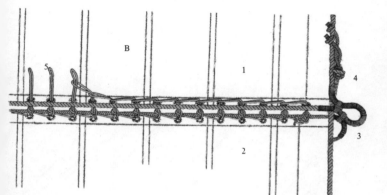

C   *Enlargement of clew of sail, showing details*

D   *Sectional view of a reefed sail*

1   Foot of sail
2   Reef band
3   Reef point
4   Reef point knotted around reef with a reef knot
5   Rolled-up canvas in reef

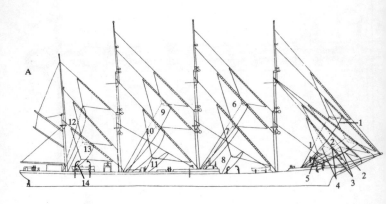

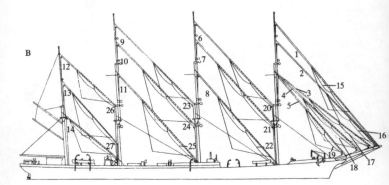

RUNNING GEAR OF STAYSAILS IN A FOUR-MASTED
BARK, DIFFERENT TYPES OF STAYSAILS

A   *Sheets*
1   Fore royal
    staysail sheets
2   Flying jib sheets
3   Outer jib sheets
4   Inner jib sheets
5   Fore topmast
    staysail sheets
6   Main royal
    staysail sheet
7   Main topgallant
    staysail sheet
8   Main topmast
    staysail sheet
9   Mizzen royal
    staysail sheet
10 Mizzen
    topgallant
    staysail sheet
11 Mizzen topmast
    staysail sheet
12 Jigger topgallant
    staysail sheet
13 Jigger topmast
    staysail sheet
14 Jigger staysail
    sheet
B   *Halliards and
    downhauls*
1   Fore royal
    staysail halliards
2   Flying jib
    halliards
3   Outer jib
    halliards
4   Inner jib
    halliards
5   Fore topmast
    staysail halliards
6   Main royal
    staysail halliards
7   Main topgallant
    staysail halliards
8   Main topmast
    staysail halliards
9   Mizzen royal
    staysail halliards
10 Mizzen
    topgallant
    staysail halliards

11 Mizzen topmast
    staysail halliards
12 Jigger topgallant
    staysail halliards
13 Jigger topmast
    staysail halliards
14 Jigger staysail
    halliards
15 Fore royal
    staysail downhaul
16 Flying jib
    downhaul
17 Outer jib
    downhaul
18 Inner jib
    downhaul
19 Fore topmast
    staysail downhaul
20 Main royal
    staysail downhaul
21 Main topgallant
    staysail downhaul
22 Main topmast
    staysail downhaul
23 Mizzen royal
    staysail downhaul
24 Mizzen
    topgallant
    staysail downhaul
25 Mizzen topmast
    staysail downhaul
26 Jigger topgallant
    staysail downhaul
27 Jigger topmast
    staysail downhaul
28 Jigger staysail
    downhaul

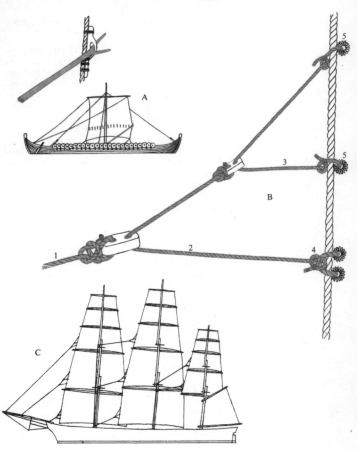

SAIL DETAILS

A *Norse Viking
    ship beating with
    a spar, known as
    a beatas, to hold
    the weather leech
    instead of a
    bowline; detail
    showing the
    spar's connection
    to sail*

B *Detail of a
    bowline bridle*
1 Bowline hitched
    to the dead block
    with a bowline
2 Long bridle
3 Short bridle
4 Bowline cringle
    in sail
5 Eyelet-holes in
    sail for short bri-
    dle

C *Outline drawing
    of an American
    clipper close
    hauled on the
    port tack, with
    her weather
    bowlines picked
    out on her
    courses, topsails,
    and topgallant
    sails*

SAIL DETAILS

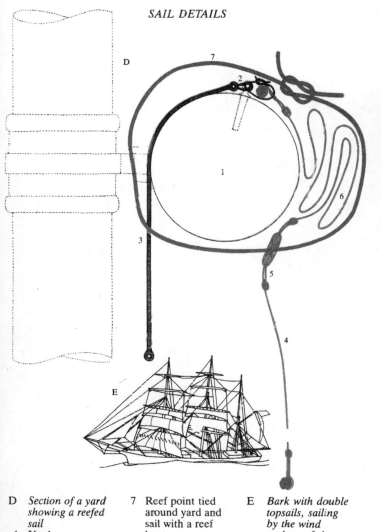

D *Section of a yard showing a reefed sail*
1 Yard
2 Jack stay
3 Stirrup
4 Sail below the reef
5 Reef band
6 Reefed part of sail

7 Reef point tied around yard and sail with a reef knot

E *Bark with double topsails, sailing by the wind under reefed upper topsails, lower topsails, and foresail*

171

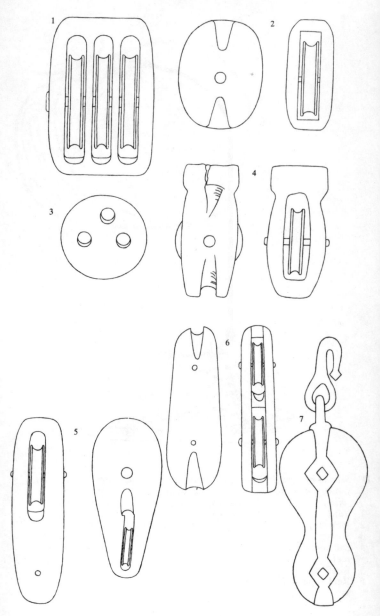

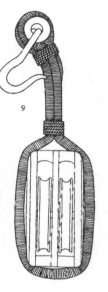
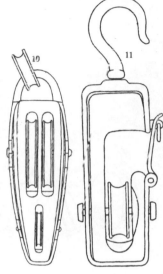

BLOCKS OF DIFFERENT TYPES

1 Triple block for a hemp strop, 19th century

2 Single block, side view and front view, for a hemp strop, 18th century

3 Deadeye, 19th century

4 Clewgarnet block, side view and front view; this block has been turned on a lathe; medieval or 16th century

5 Dutch style yard-arm sheet block for topsail sheet and lower lift, front view and side view, 17th century

6 Fiddleblock, side view and front view, with two sheaves, 18th or 19th century

7 Fiddleblock, with external strap and hook, 19th century

8 Wire-stropped sheet block, with clip hooks and a cleat for the sheet, so as to make the sheet block travel on a horse, 20th century

9 Double block with a double strop and hook, for masthead pendant, 19th century

10 Triple fiddleblock, with external strap and thimble for splicing the pendant, 19th century

11 Snatch block, with external straps and a swivel hook, 19th century

173

TACKLES AND BLOCKS

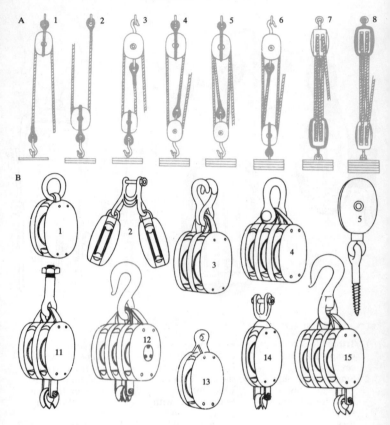

TACKLES AND BLOCKS

A *Tackles (the number of loads indicates the increase of power for each tackle)*
1 Single whip
2 Runner
3 Gun tackle
4 Gun tackle rove to advantage
5 Luff tackle
6 Luff tackle rove to advantage
7 Double purchase

8 Double purchase rove to advantage
9 Winding tackle
10 Reversed winding tackle
11 Triple tackle
12 Reversed triple tackle
13 Four-by-three tackle
14 Three-by-four tackle
15 Four-fold tackle
16 Quadruple tackle

B *Different blocks with internal iron straps*
1 Single block with a ring
2 Fore-and-aft jib sheet block
3 Double block with sister hooks
4 Triple block with a shackle
5 Single block with loose swivel screw eye bolt

174

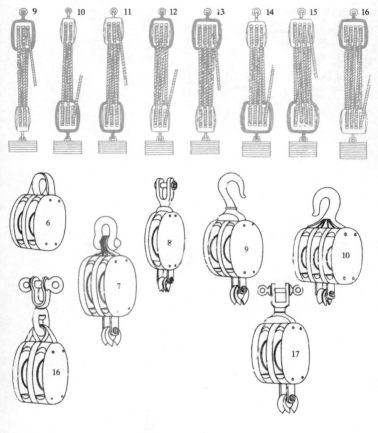

6 Double block with an eye
7 Double block with shackle and becket
8 Single block with stiff swivel jaws and becket
9 Double block with stiff swivel hook and becket
10 Triple block with stiff fixed front hook and becket

11 Double block with eye bolt and nut and becket
12 Triple block with loose side hook and becket
13 Single block with a solid eye for gaff bands
14 Single block with stiff jaws and becket

15 Triple block with loose swivel hook and becket
16 Double block with loose swivel jaws with guy eyes
17 Double block with stiff swivel jaws with guy eyes and becket

SOME OLD RIGGING DETAILS

A *Topsail, halliard,
    end of 17th cen-
    tury*
1 Tie
2 Tackle
3 Lower lift

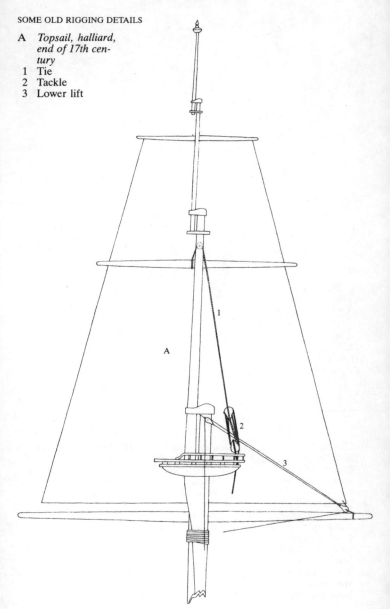

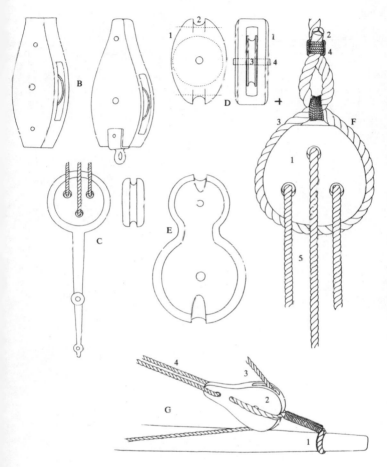

B *Wooden blocks without strops*
C *Chain plate with deadeye*
D *Block for hemp strop*
1 Shell
2 Score for the strop
3 Sheave
4 Pin

E *Fiddleblock with one sheave smaller than the other*
F *Deadeye, turned in a shroud*
1 Deadeye
2 Shroud
3 Throat-seizing
4 End-seizing
5 Lanyard

G *Lower yardarm with topsail sheet block*
1 Lower yardarm
2 Topsail sheet block
3 Topsail sheet
4 Lower lift

177

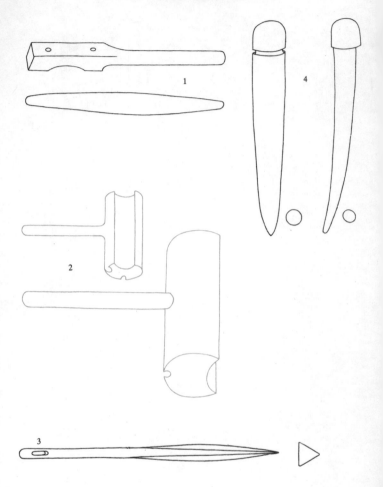

TOOLS FOR SAIL-MAKING AND RIGGING WORK

1 Turning fids or heavers
2 Serving mallets
3 Big sail needle, roping needle
4 Splicing fids
5 Carved bullock's horn with tallow for holding needles
6 Prickers for small work
7 Marlinespikes for splicing wire
8 Sail-maker's palm

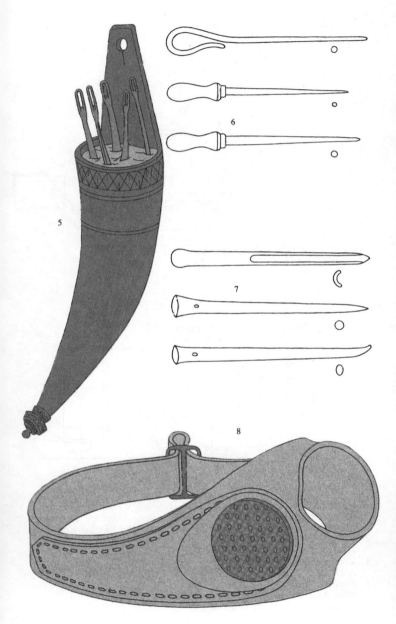

5

6

7

8

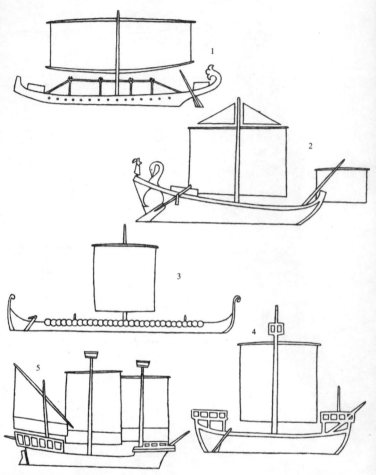

OLD TYPES OF SAILING SHIPS

1 Egyptian sea-
  going ship, about
  1500 B.C.
2 Roman trader,
  about A.D. 200
3 Viking longship,
  A.D. 900
4 Norman ship
  from the 13th
  century

5 Hulk of the Han-
  seatic League,
  about 1470
6 Spanish caravel,
  about 1490
7 Spanish ship,
  nao,
  about 1490
8 English carrack,
  about 1500

9 North European
  boeier, 1560
10 Swedish kravel,
  galleon, 1550

180

OLD TYPES OF SAILING SHIPS

1 Dutch pinnace,
  middle of 17th
  century

2 Swedish packet,
  1690

3 Algerian chebec,
  18th century

4 Dutch flute, 1640

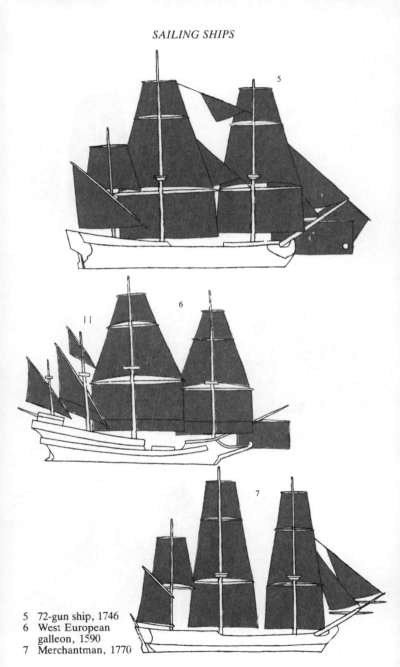

5 72-gun ship, 1746
6 West European
   galleon, 1590
7 Merchantman, 1770

OLD TYPES OF SAILING SHIPS

1 Swedish krayer, second half of 18th century
2 Hooker, second half of 18th century
3 Swedish East Indiaman, 1786

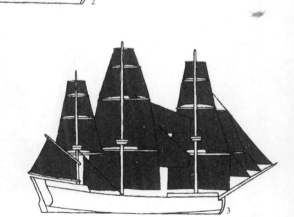

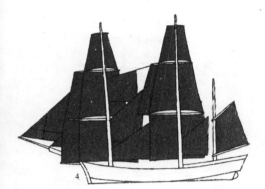

4 Swedish bark, 1792
5 Swedish snow, 1783
6 Baltimore clipper, 1820

185

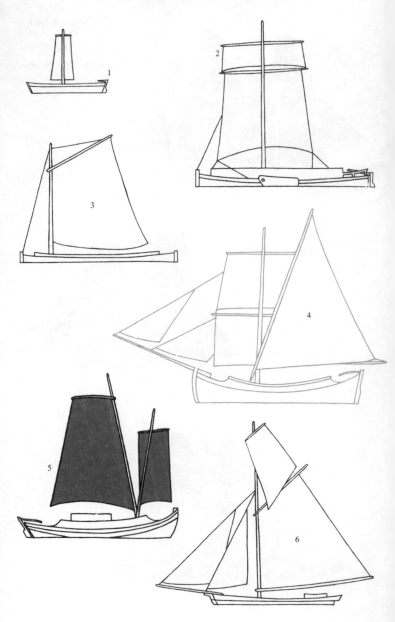

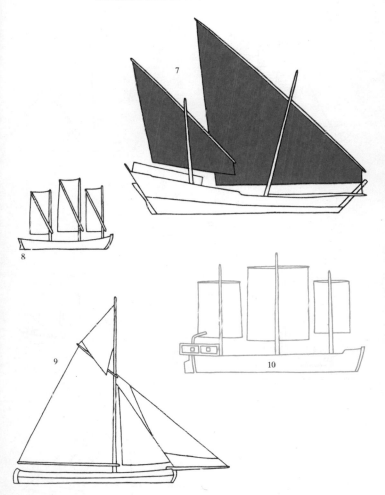

SOME ETHNOGRAPHICAL BOAT TYPES

1 Boat from the Göta River, West Sweden
2 Humber keel, Yorkshire
3 Norfolk wherry
4 Turkish caïque
5 Boat from Bahia, Brazil
6 Sloop from archipelago off Stockholm
7 Arabian dhow
8 Fishing boat from the Åland Islands, Finland
9 Danish revenue cutter
10 Old barge, Lake of Vänern, Sweden

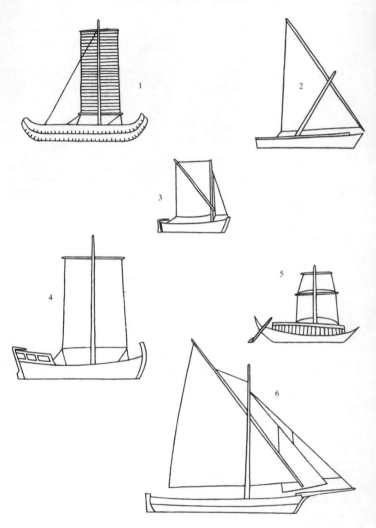

SOME ETHNOGRAPHICAL BOAT TYPES

1 Reed-boat from Lake Titicaca, South America
2 Boat from Lake Victoria
3 Small fishing boat from west coast of Sweden
4 Norwegian jacht
5 Boat from East Pakistan
6 Tartan, trading craft from western Mediterranean

7 Koster boat from west coast of Sweden
8 Piragua from Tahiti
9 Portuguese muleta
10 Boat from Kimari, India
11 Outrigger canoe from the South Pacific
12 Dutch barge

SOME ETHNOGRAPHICAL BOAT
TYPES

1 Dutch koff
2 Scow schooner,
   New Zealand
3 Junk, Amoy,
   South China

4 Paduakan, coasting craft from Celebes
5 Bovo, Sicilian coaster
6 Ketch, Åland Islands, Finland

191

SOME ETHNOGRAPHICAL BOAT TYPES

1 Velocera,
   Sicilian, lateen-
   rigged barkentine
2 Egyptian markab
3 Bilancella,
   Italian fishing
   craft
4 Thames barge

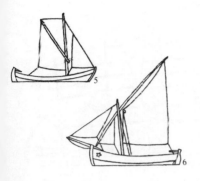

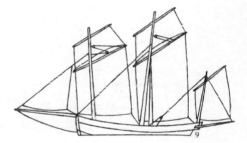

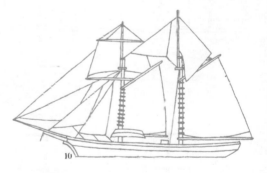

5 German *Heuer* boat	8 Small Norwegian sailing fishing boat	10 French Grand Banks schooner
6 Greek fishing boat from Mykonos	9 French lugger (*chasse marée*)	
7 Open Spanish fishing boat (*felucca*)		

193

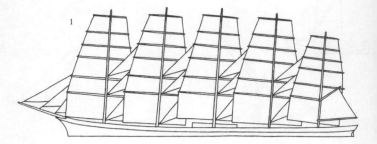

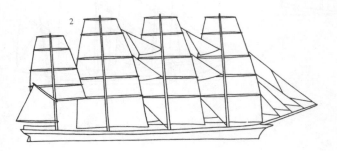

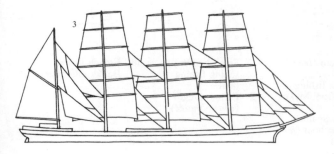

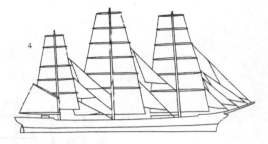

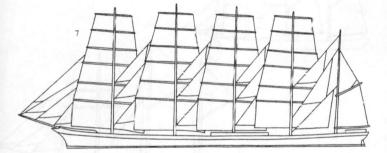

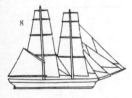

DIFFERENT RIGS

1 Five-masted ship	5 Snow	8 Brig
2 Four-masted ship	6 Main topsail	9 Bark
3 Four-masted bark	brigantine	
4 Ship	7 Five-masted bark	

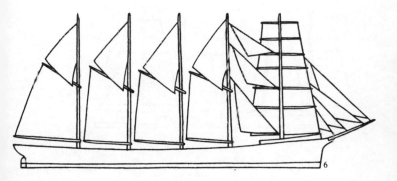

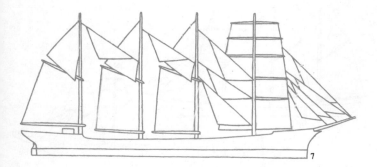

DIFFERENT RIGS

1 Brigantine or
   hermaphrodite
   brig
2 Four-masted
   jackass bark
3 Jackass bark
4 Barkentine

5 Six-masted
   barkentine
6 Five-masted
   barkentine
7 Four-masted
   barkentine

DIFFERENT RIGS

1 Five-masted two-
   topsail schooner
2 Four-masted top-
   sail schooner
3 Three-masted
   topsail schooner
4 Main-topsail
   schooner or two-
   topsail schooner
5 Topsail schooner
6 Seven-masted
   fore-and-aft
   schooner

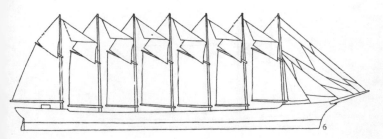

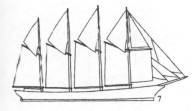

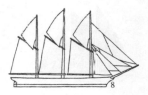

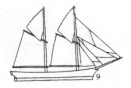

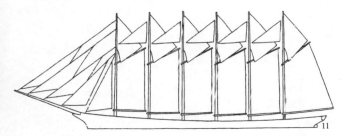

7 Four-masted
   fore-and-aft
   schooner rigged
   with a flying
   foresail

8 Three-masted
   fore-and-aft
   schooner
9 Two-masted fore-
   and-aft schooner

10 Three-masted
    staysail schooner
11 Six-masted fore-
    and-aft schooner

199

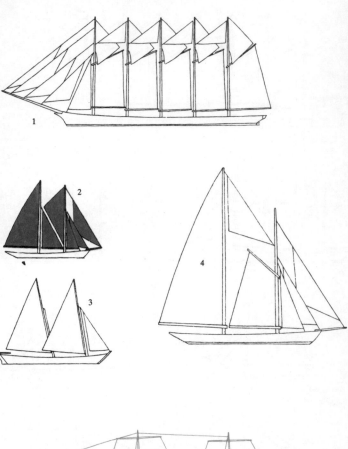

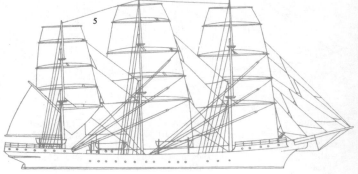

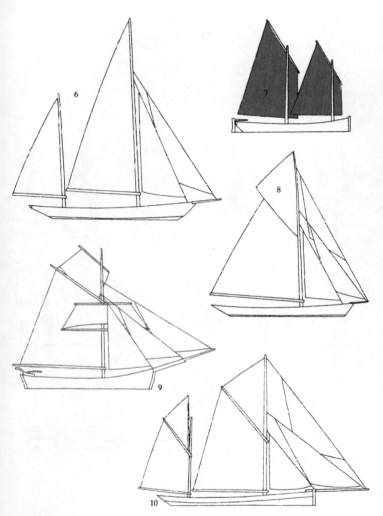

DIFFERENT RIGS

1   Five-masted fore-and-aft
    schooner
2   Two-masted staysail
    schooner
3   Gunter-rigged gig
4   Two-masted schooner
    with Bermuda mainsail

5   Training ship DENMARK
6   Bermuda-rigged ketch
7   Launch rigged with dip-
    ping lugsails
8   Gaff-rigged cutter
9   Baltic sloop
10 Ketch

KNOTS

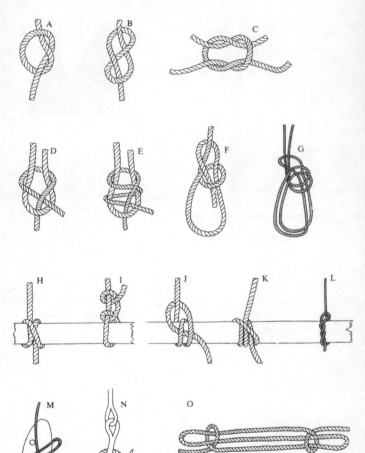

KNOTS, WHIPPINGS, AND SPLICE

A	Overhand knot	D	Sheet bend	H	Clove hitch
B	Figure of eight knot, Flemish knot	E	Double sheet bend, variation	I	Two half-hitches
		F	Bowline	J	Fisherman's bend
C	Square knot, reef knot	G	Bowline on the bight	K	Rolling hitch
				L	Timber hitch
				M	Slippery hitch

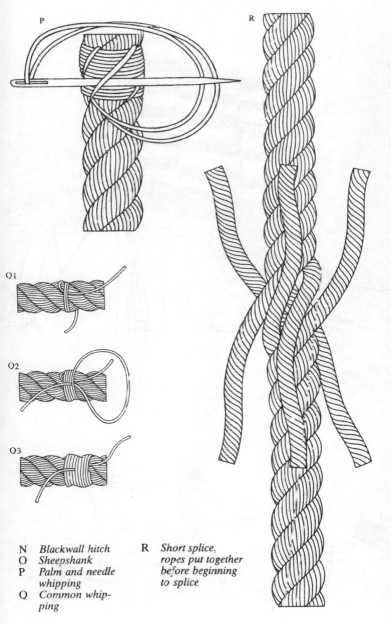

N *Blackwall hitch*
O *Sheepshank*
P *Palm and needle whipping*
Q *Common whipping*

R *Short splice, ropes put together before beginning to splice*

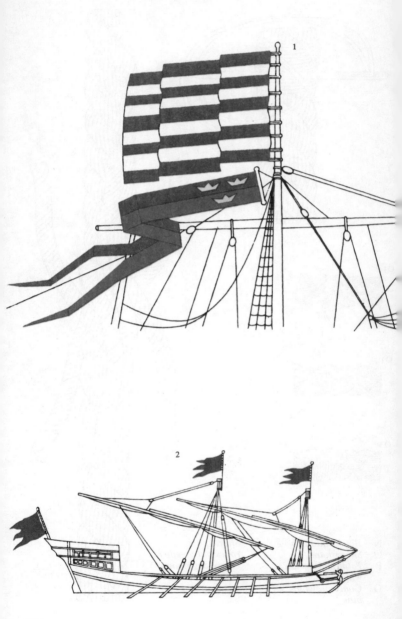

SWEDISH FLAGS

1 In the second half of the 16th century the present Swedish flag was not yet in use. Instead Swedish men-of-war flew a blue-and-white striped flag.
The pennant at the masthead, however, carried the three Swedish crowns.

2 The three-tongued blue flag of the fleet of the army, 1761–1813

3 The ensign of 1658, from the oldest preserved Swedish flag, now in the Rijksmuseum, Amsterdam

4 Merchant flag, 1815–1844, with the canton of the Swedish-Norwegian Union

5 The ensign with the canton of the Union, 1844–1905

6 Merchant flag, after 1905

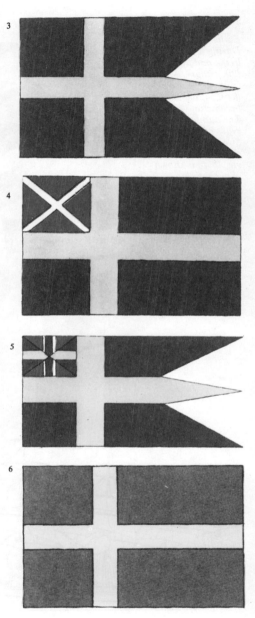

SIGNAL FLAGS

*Earlier signal systems
During a few decades
in the middle of the
19th century, Marryat's
code was in use before
the Commercial Code
became universal.
The number in Mar-
ryat's code of the
Swedish three-masted
ship* Indiaman *of Gä-
vle, 1856, is shown
above the ship.*

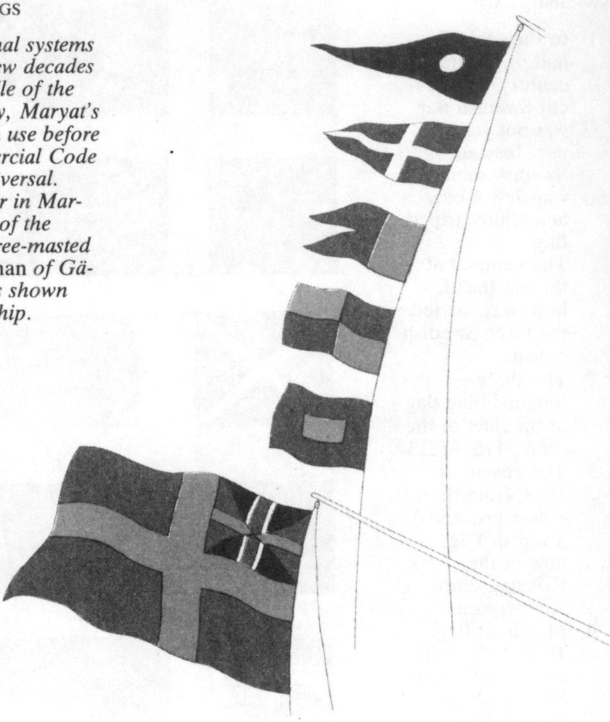

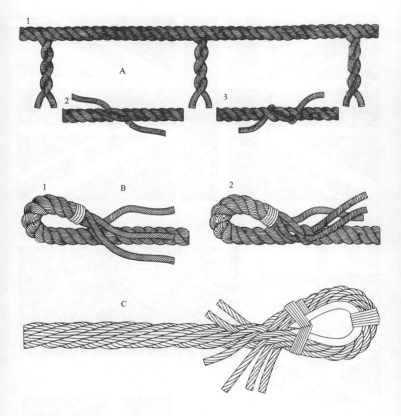

SPLICES

When splicing cordage the strands are tucked against the lay. Each strand is taken over the strand on its left and then under the next one.

A *Long splice*
1 The ropes laid up before beginning to splice

2 Way of knotting the strands
3 Way of tucking the strands

B *Eye splice*
1 Way of placing the strand before commencing the splice
2 Way of tucking the two first strands

C *Eye splice on a wire rope, one tuck made on each strand.*

When splicing wire rope each strand is generally tucked around the same strand all the time, in the same direction, as the single wires are laid.

207

A1

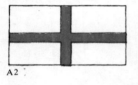

A2

A5

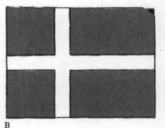

A3

A4

B

A *Great Britain*
1 Union flag
2 Cross of St. George
3 Cross of St. Andrew
4 Cross of St. Patrick

5 Merchant flag (red ensign)
B According to a legend, the Danish flag fell from the sky in front of the army in 1219 and led

the army to victory. It is probably the oldest flag in the world, and has been Denmark's colors since the 14th century.

FLAGS

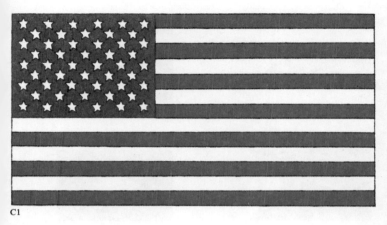

C1

C2

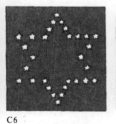

C3

C4

C5   C6   C7

C	*United States of America*	2	The 13 stars of 1777	No official design for placement of the stars existed before 1912
1	The U.S. flag of today. The stars represent the 50 states and the stripes the original 13 states	3	1795	
		4	1818	
		5	1846	
		6	1848	
		7	1912	

209

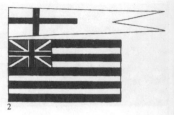

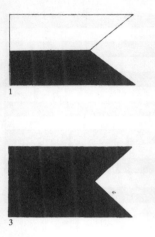

FLAGS

House flags from sailing ship days
1 The Hanseatic League, Lübeck (the Middle Ages)
2 The East India Company, London
3 Black Ball Line, New York (1816)
4 Enoch Train White Diamond Line, Boston (1820's)
5 Grinnell, Minturn & Co., New York, Swallow Tail Line for Liverpool
6 Grinnell, Minturn & Co., New York, Swallow Tail Line for London
7 Arthur Sewall, Bath, Me.
8 Alaska Packers Association, San Francisco
9 Money Wigram & Sons, London
10 George Thompson & Co., Aberdeen White Star Line, Aberdeen
11 John Willis & Son, London
12 Devitt & Moore, London
13 John Hardie & Co., Glasgow
14 Thomas Law & Co., Shire Line, Glasgow
15 John Stewart & Co., London
16 Andrew Weir & Co., Bank Line, Glasgow
17 Soc. Anon. Des Voiliers Nantais, Nantes
18 Ferdinand Laeisz, Hamburg
19 S.O. Stray & Co., Kristiansand
20 Gustaf Erikson, Mariehamn

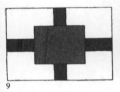

An old engraving shows Magellan during his trip around the world, 1519–1522. Magellan was never able to complete this first circumnavigation of the globe himself, and of the original five vessels, with 265 men in the crew, only one ship, the VIC- TORIA, and eighteen men returned. The engraving introduces the chapter on naviga- tion and ship-hand- ling.

NAVIGATION AND SHIP-HANDLING
by Rolf Scheen

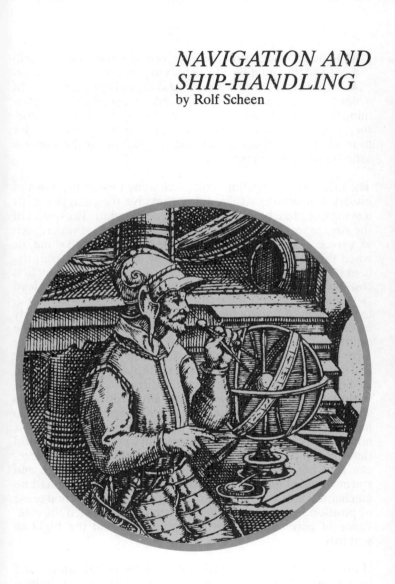

T he art of determining the position and course of a ship and thus guiding it from port to port is known as navigation, from the Latin *navis,* a ship, and *agere,* to drive. In order to navigate successfully, the sailor must be able to determine three things: *(1)* the actual position of the ports of departure and destination; *(2)* the course the ship must take in order to reach its port of destination safely; *(3)* how far the ship has sailed since leaving port.

The first act of navigation took place some time in the dawn of history and probably then did not involve the primitive craft leaving one place bound for a specific destination. The object of the voyage was, almost certainly, to cross a body of water, such as a river, a lake, or a bay. When the urge to explore came, or when the need to find food, game, or living space arose, the land on the other side of the water was one of the places first considered. Once it had been established that it was indeed possible to cross over the water in the primitive craft available, the problem of finding the way home arose. And if the newly explored land was considered to be worth returning to, the sailor would want to be able to find it again. Just as migratory birds have developed the ability to find their way south in winter and north in summer, always to the same places, year after year, so did early man develop his sense of direction and perception, so that he could find his way without any mechanical aids. This ability is noticeable even today in older fishermen who seem to have developed the ability to "smell" their way round their home waters. But it is among the primitive peoples of the world that this ability is best seen today. The Eskimo, for instance, can find his way home in his kayak through darkness and storms, guided only by his instinct. Early sailors, who had no mechanical aids to guide them, developed this instinctual sense of position, assisted by a keen perception that noted the relevance of current flow, flotsam from land, and the flight of seabirds.

However, even if we consider the sailors of the Stone and Bronze Ages to have been excellent practitioners of primitive navigation, no real step forward in the art could be achieved until the science of mathematics had advanced considerably. And although astronomy was considered a science in Babylon in the third millennium before our era, and Chinese scholars could compute the occurrence of solar eclipses, this knowledge was not applied to navigation. One reason for this could be that at that time there was no pressing need for such development, as most shipping that took place then consisted of river traffic. It was first the Phoenicians and then the Greeks who began sailing out of sight of land and therefore needed to develop navigation as a science.

For a long time, however, coastal navigation remained the dominant form of shipping in the Mediterranean basin. By coastal navigation is meant that the ship, if at all possible, never went out of sight of land, the sailor's most important navigational instrument being, therefore, the eyes.

The first navigational aid to be developed was the lead and line, and this is recorded in ancient Egypt, where shipping on the Nile represented a vital means of transport. The Nile waters can be so turbid that it is impossible to see the bottom, and annual flooding alters the river's course so that banks and shoals change place regularly. Therefore, the Nile rivermen had to be able to sound the river. Some ancient depictions of Egyptian boats show a man in the prow using a long pole to measure the depth of the water. On larger boats, the hull's height above the water made poles impractical, and the lead and line came into use. In the year 62 A.D., the ship that foundered when taking the apostle Paul as prisoner to Rome is recorded as having a lead. By that time, the lead was so developed that the line was marked in fathoms.

The main object of the lead was to save the ship from going aground. Once the position of a shoal or bank was known, it could be avoided. Landmarks, or transit marks, were noted, so that transit lines could be followed, thus keeping the ship clear of danger. Transit lines are used today still in coastal navigation.

Once the art of writing became widespread, information about navigational dangers was gathered and noted down for use by mariners. Greek and Phoenician scholars were especially proficient at this, writing down sailing directions and navigational information on what were called *peripli*. Herodotus (c. 450 B.C.) tells us that King Darius I of Persia hired Phoenician ships to spy on the Greek coast and to make up a set of sailing

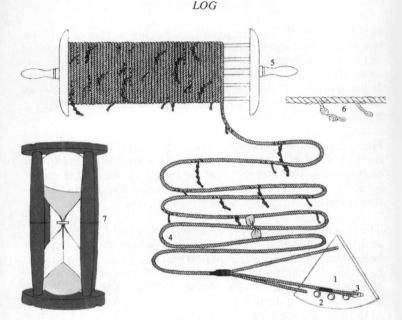

THE OLD LOG WITH A LINE AND GLASS

The chip log is an old instrument for measuring the speed of a ship. It consists of a flat piece of wood formed as a sector of a circle and weighted to enable it to float upright, secured to a line so as to make it float square. When thrown overboard it will remain stationary in the water and, as the ship sails away, the measured line will reel off at a corresponding rate. An hourglass determines the fixed interval of time, and the length of line run out will measure the speed

of the ship. A quick pull on the line will detach the peg in the log chip, making it float flat so it can be hauled in.

1 The log, known as the wood float or chip
2 Lead pellets holding the chip vertically in the water
3 Wooden peg, which allows the chip to float flat when it is pulled out
4 Log-line measured off in "knots," having a similar relation to a nautical mile

as the trickle of sand in the hourglass has to one hour
5 Log reel
6 Mark for two knots and a plain mark for half a knot
7 Hourglass, log glass, running for 28 seconds. A 14-second glass is used for speeds over 8 knots

directions for his navy, for use when it would be navigating Greek waters.

Later on, sea charts became more important than sailing directions, but they could not become truly useful until the invention and widespread acceptance of the compass. The first known map of the world to have a grid of lengthwise and crosswise lines was that drawn by Eratosthenes, who was head of the famous Library at Alexandria in the second century B.C. Map-making developed through the centuries, and in 1569, Gerard Mercator, a Flemish cartographer, invented a special grid called the Mercator projection, which he used when drawing maps. On the Mercator projection, the globe is represented as a cylinder with the lines of longitude parallel to each other. As a result, it was possible to draw a correct course line between two points on the map. The scale of the map varied from the Equator to the poles, so that at 60 degrees North or South, for instance, one nautical mile on the chart had twice the length of the nautical mile at the Equator. In the neighborhood of the poles, the Mercator projection cannot be used at all.

On a map, the distance from the Equator to the poles is divided into 90 degrees of latitude (North or South). The Equator itself is divided into 360 degrees of longitude, with a vertical (a meridian, or a line of longitude) stretching from each degree to the poles. In the beginning, no 0-meridian was considered standard, and each country placed it where they thought fit, often picking their own capital city as the point through which the 0-meridian passed. In 1634, King Louis XIII of France decreed that the 0-meridian was to be considered as passing through the island of Ferro, the most westerly of the Canary Islands, then regarded as the Old World's most westerly point. This was used internationally until 1884, when it was agreed that the 0-meridian was to be considered as passing through the Greenwich Observatory (founded in 1675), which is situated in the outskirts of London.

In ancient times, a great deal of courage was required of mariners who ventured so far out to sea that the land "fell away" from view. No reliable charts existed then; nor did the compass. Perhaps it was a combination of good weather, the spirit of adventure, curiosity, and the improving seaworthiness

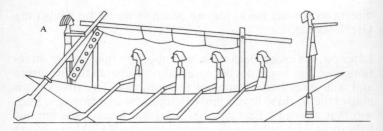

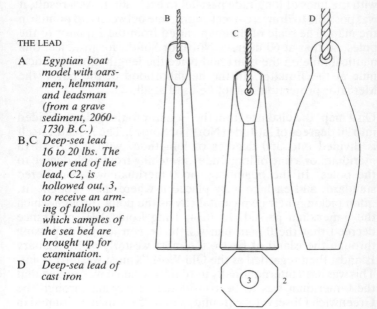

THE LEAD

A   *Egyptian boat model with oarsmen, helmsman, and leadsman (from a grave sediment, 2060-1730 B.C.)*

B,C *Deep-sea lead 16 to 20 lbs. The lower end of the lead, C2, is hollowed out, 3, to receive an arming of tallow on which samples of the sea bed are brought up for examination.*

D   *Deep-sea lead of cast iron*

HAND LEAD AND LINE

The lead is the sailor's oldest navigational in-strument, known even in ancient Egypt. It consists of a lead weight and a meas-ured line, which is used to determine the depth of water. For different depths, leads of different weights were used, but today the deep-sea lead is replaced by sounding machines or echo sounders. The

hand lead is still used occasionally in shallow water. The line used to be 20 fathoms long, and in the Royal British Navy it is marked in the following way:

2 fathoms: two strips of leather
3 fathoms: three strips of leather
5 fathoms: a piece of white duck
7 fathoms: a piece of red bunting

10 fathoms: a piece of leather with a hole in it
13 fathoms: a piece of blue serge
15 fathoms: a piece of white duck
17 fathoms: a piece of red bunting
20 fathoms: a piece of house line with two knots

NAVIGATIONAL INSTRUMENTS

OLD NAVIGATIONAL INSTRUMENTS

A Astrolabe, con-
structed by the
Arabs in the 10th
century, and
used, mostly by
the Spaniards
and Portuguese,
up to the 17th
century. It con-
sists of a freely
suspended gradu-
ated ring with a
diametrical ruler
holding two sight
vanes through
which the sun or
a star may be ob-
served, the alti-
tude being read
off on the circle.

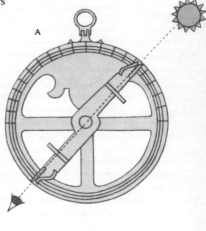

B The fore staff is
composed of a
square staff and
three vanes of
different lengths.
The sides of the
staff have
different scales,
each correspond-
ing to one of the
vanes. When ob-
serving the alti-
tude of the sun
(star) only one
vane is used.
Holding one end
of the staff to his
eye, the observer
moves the vane
until he sees its
lower end level
with the horizon
and the upper
end in one with
the sun. The alti-
tude is read off
where the vane
cuts the staff.

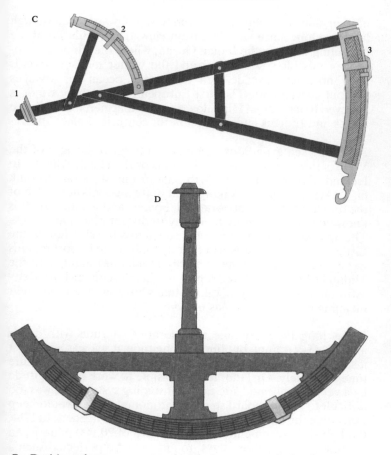

C   Davis' quadrant is composed of two arcs of a circle having the same center and three vanes: the horizon vane (1) with a slot, the shade vane (2), and the sight vane (3) with a sight hole. The horizon vane is fixed at the center, the other two vanes run upon the arcs. The quadrant is used with the observer's back to the sun. The shade vane is set at a suitable number of degrees, and the observer moves the sight vane until he observes the sun's shadow in one with the horizon, as seen through the slot in the horizon vane.

D   Gunter's quadrant is made on the same principles as the Davis' quadrant, and it is used with the observer's back to the sun.

221

of their ships that persuaded them to sail onward, even though land had long since vanished from view. The regularity of the prevailing winds in the Indian Ocean, where the summer monsoon winds blow south-west and the winter monsoon winds blow north-east, made it a favourable ocean for voyages without instruments. The first European to use these winds is believed to have been Hippalos, a Greek mariner, although the Arabs and Indians had used them for centuries before that.

As daring sea expeditions, however, the great voyages of the Vikings through the mists and storms of the North Atlantic to Iceland, Greenland, and North America must be said to rank high. Admittedly, the Vikings had quite a good knowledge of the movements of the celestial bodies and could use this knowledge in navigating their way to distant places and back. The apparent movements of the sun across the sky, and of the Little Dipper and the North Star by night were important aids in helping them navigate. The bright summer nights and the Midnight Sun also played a part in Viking seamanship. Many astronomical terms from Viking times have survived, but their meaning is lost in the mists of time.

It has long been possible to determine latitude with a fair amount of certainty, but finding longitude at sea was an almost insoluble problem due to the lack of an instrument to measure time accurately. On land, it was possible to work out longitude by a very complicated and time-consuming system that was too difficult to use on board ship. A chronometer that would keep exact time throughout a long ocean voyage was needed. In 1714, the British government offered a reward of 20,000 pounds, an enormous sum in those days, to anyone who perfected such a chronometer. In 1759, John Harrison, a Yorkshire clockmaker, perfected a marine chronometer that was tested on two voyages to Jamaica. After six weeks at sea, the clock erred by only five seconds. With Harrison's chronometer, a revolution in navigation took place; from then on, it was possible to determine the longitude of a ship's position at sea. In 1774, Harrison received the prize for his great contribution to navigation.

The most important innovation in the history of navigation is much older, however, and this is the invention of the compass. The first use of the magnetic compass has been attributed to the ancient Chinese of the Hsia Dynasty (*c.* 2600 B.C.), although this now seems unlikely. The earliest Chinese reference to the use of a compass on board a ship seems to be in a document from 1111 A.D., and it is possible that the Chinese had their first contact with the compass from Indian seamen. According to Are Frode, the Vikings used a *leiderstein* (lodestone) as a primitive compass during a voyage from Norway to Iceland in 868 A.D. Considering the huge quantities of magnetite to be found in Norway, it is not unreasonable to suppose that the Norwegians discovered its properties at an early stage and had conceived the idea of using magnetite aboard ship to help them to establish the position of North.

Celestial navigation is based upon the measurement of the altitude of celestial bodies and the determination of their position. All ships measuring the height of the same celestial body at the same time and finding the same height are placed on the same astronomical position line. This fact can be used to establish position according to principles first laid down in 1837 by the American naval officer, Thomas H. Sumner, and further amplified by Marc St. Hilaire around 1875. Many different instruments have, in the course of time, been invented to measure the altitude of celestial bodies: the quadrant is said to have been invented by the Greek astronomer Hipparchos as early as the year 150 B.C. The Jacob's staff, or the cross-staff, was invented by Levi Ben Gerson from Catalonia in 1342. John Hadley constructed the Hadley quadrant in 1731, and this was soon developed into the sextant by the British naval officer Campbell in 1757.

A number of computed tables is necessary in order to establish position through celestial navigation. Such tables were first published in 1475 under the title *Ephemerides Astronomicae* by Regiomontanus. In 1755, Tobias Mayer, a German scientist living in Göttingen, edited tables necessary for establishing Greenwich Mean Time. Then, in 1767, the *British Nautical Almanac* was compiled by Nevil Maskelyne, the Astronomer Royal, and it has been published regularly since then.

When laying a course, the navigator must draw a line from the position of the port of departure to that of the port of destination. The course can then be read by placing a compass along

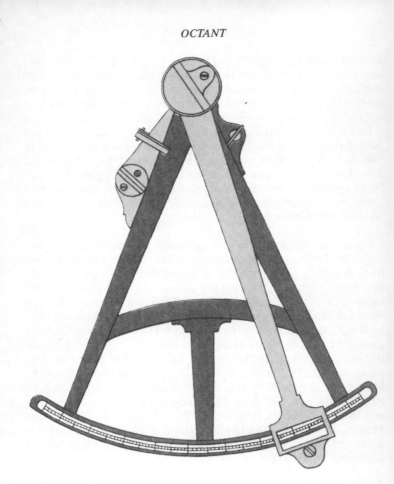

OCTANT AND SEXTANT

Hadley's octant, invented in 1731, and a forerunner of the sextant. The octant brought the art of measuring altitudes at sea to theoretical perfection, and later improvements are due to better methods of manufacturing only.

The sextant (opposite) is an improvement on Hadley's octant, which is said to have been invented in 1731. The sextant is a portable, reflecting astronomical instrument for measuring angles. When used, it can be held in the hand without a stand, which is essential on

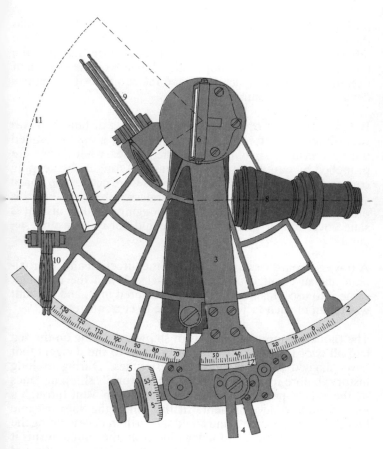

board ships at sea.
*The instrument cons-
ists of a sector-shaped
frame with a gradu-
ated arc of a circle.
Pivoted at the center
of the arc is a radius
bar, which swings
across the surface of
the graduated arc.
The principal parts of
a sextant are:*

1 The frame
2 The arc, known
   as the limb
3 The index bar
4 Clamping mecha-
   nism
5 Micrometer
   screw
6 Index mirror

7 Horizon glass
8 Telescope
9 Index shades
10 Horizon shades
11 Measured angle
12 Reading of
    measured angle,
    here 45° 0'

the line, taking into account the variation caused by the fact that the geographic North Pole and the magnetic North Pole have different positions. Consideration must also be taken of the built-in magnetism of the ship, which depends on the amount of iron in the ship, her machinery, and the cargo, as this causes a deviation on the compass.

Before the advent of charts which gave exact distances, it was very difficult to determine accurately how far a ship had sailed during a certain span of time. In ancient times, when ships were propelled by oars, distance was measured roughly by keeping count of the amount of time the rowers were active. On board sailing-ships, the hand log and hourglass were used, but this only gave the speed at the time of logging, so that distances sailed over longer periods of time could not be measured accurately.

A traverse board was used to record the direction and approximate distance sailed on different tacks. When the log book came into use, this information was entered in it, and account was taken of such factors as drift due to currents, etc.

The thousands upon thousands of shipwrecks lying on the sea bed all over the world bear silent witness to the dangers that have plagued mariners since earliest times. During its long history, before it was phased out of the world's shipping lanes by the engine-powered vessel, the sailing-ship went through a long period of development. In that time, the ship became bigger, more seaworthy, and could sail farther, necessitating the development of the art of navigation from the simple forms it had in the Middle East to the advanced forms it took at the end of the era. Today, the sailing-ship is no more, but the art of navigation has progressed beyond the wildest dreams of the early mariners, with the use of electronics and satellites, while the word "navigation" now means the science of determining position and course on land, on water, in the air, and in space.

COMPASS CARDS

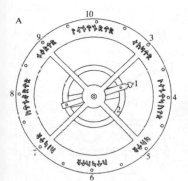

A

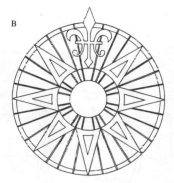

B

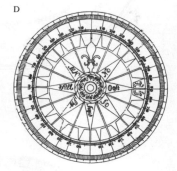

C

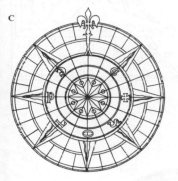

D

OLD COMPASS CARDS

A *Compass, 13th century
Reconstruction of a Scandinavian compass (leidarstein) with a bronze bowl and a wooden float, with a lodestone to point the compass*

1 Lid forming a cross with a center hole controlling the float

2 Float with lodestone
3 AUSTR. east
4 LANDSUDR, southeast
5 SUDR, south
6 UTSUDR, southwest
7 VESTR, west
8 UTNORDR, northwest
9 NORDR, north
10 LANDNORDR, northeast

B *Compass card, 1345*
C *Compass card, 1545*
D *Compass card, end of the 18th century*

227

A

B

C

**EARLY NAVIGATIONAL
INSTRUMENTS**

A *Pocket sun-dial,
1453. The indica-
tor, which cast
the sun's shadow
on the figures, is
under the lid in
the middle.*

B *Nocturnal, 1580,
to tell the time
from the stars.*

C *Traverse board,
to record the
direction and dis-
tance made on
tacks during a
watch.*

229

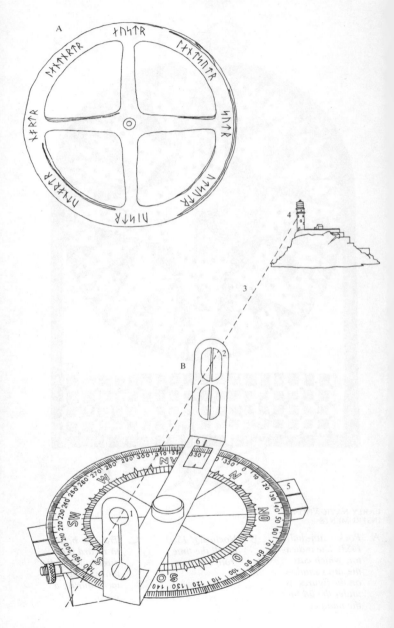

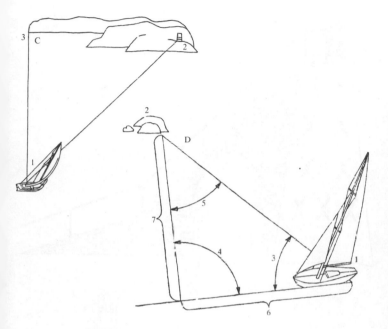

BEARINGS

A *Reconstruction of a compass card from the Viking Age*
B *Pelorus*
1, 2 Sight vanes
3 Position line
4 Object
5 Fore-and-aft mark to which the ship's course on the pelorus is clamped
6 Compass bearing
C *Cross bearing*
The exact position of the ship (1) will be known if bearings of two objects (2 and 3) are taken at the same time

D *Distance by four-point bearing*
When a fixed object (2) is bearing 45 degrees on the bow (3) note the time or log. Then the same course is steered until the object bears on the beam, or 90 degrees from the course (4). The distance (6) run by the ship (1) in the interval is the distance (7) of the object when abeam. This is clear from the fact that the ship's course and

the two bearings form an isosceles triangle (3, 4, 5), where the two sides (6, 7) are equal.

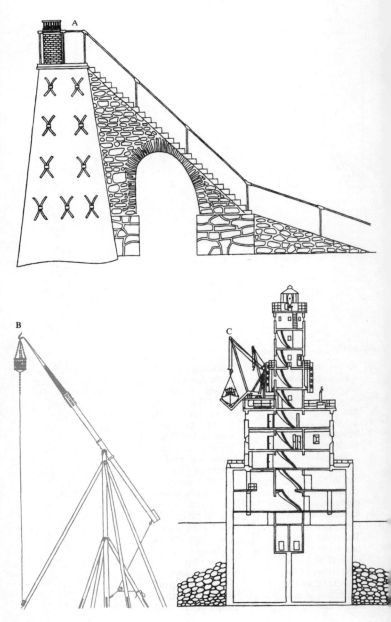

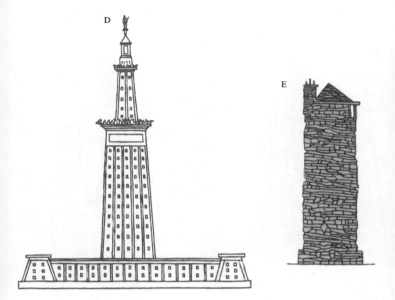

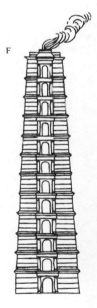

LIGHTHOUSES

A   *Open coal fire at Djursten, Sweden, 1765*
B   *Fire on tilting spar, 1635*
C   *Modern caisson lighthouse, built of concrete on shore, launched, and towed to its station and there sunk*
D   *Pharos at Alexandria, 390 B.C.*
E   *Torre de Herculum at Coruna, at the time of Christ*
F   *Tour d'Ordre at Boulogne, A.D. 40*

233

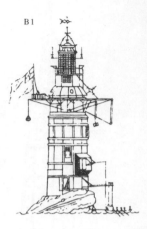

A *Cordouan at the mouth of Girande estuary in France, 1610*
B *Eddystone light in the Channel*
1 1698 (at low water)
2 1759 (at low water)
3 1882 (at high water)

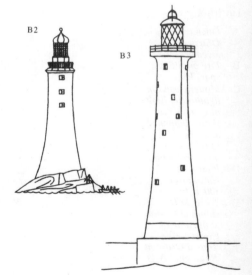

234

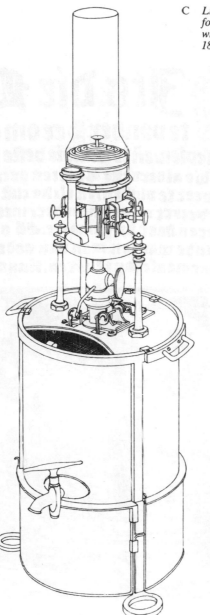

C *Lighthouse lamp
for paraffin oil
with 4 wicks,
1880's*

A

Its die Caer

te vander See om oost eñ
west te seplen/eñ is vandie beste Piloots/
eñ is wt die aloervekke Caerten gecorrigeert
diemen weet te vinden/eñ elcke cust op zijn ge
stelt/verbetert eñ vermeerdert met veel scho
ne Figueren daer up gemaect. Eñ ooc salmen
hier in vinde wat een man van node is omme
Stuermanschap te leren. Anno. 1561.

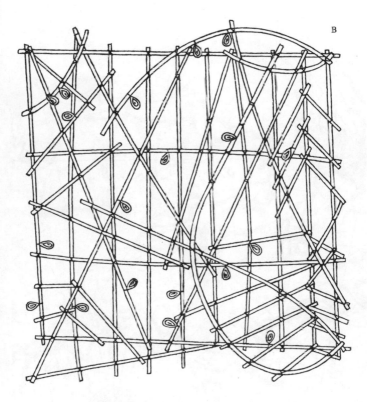

B

CHARTS

Verbal descriptions have probably existed as long as man has sailed. The oldest written "pilots" are the Greek Periples which gave distances and courses (about 300 B.C.). These were the origins of the Roman Portulanes. In the 15th and 16th centuries, "pilots" were published in most West European countries.

A   The title page of the Dutch "Het Leeskaartboek van Wisboy" (the "Chart book" from Visby), first published in 1551. Several editions followed in Dutch as well as in German. The book also contained woodcut shore views. This figure is from the edition of 1561.

B   Native chart of the Marshall Islands consisting of a framework of palmleaf veins with shells or coral pieces indicating the different islands and their relative positions. The distances between the islands were not always known, but most important were the directions.

A

CHARTS AND SURVEYING

A   *Detail from a   B   *A Swedish chart
    Swedish chart of   of the Sound,
    the Baltic, 1645*   1819; the same
                                region is shown
                                in the upper part
                                of A*

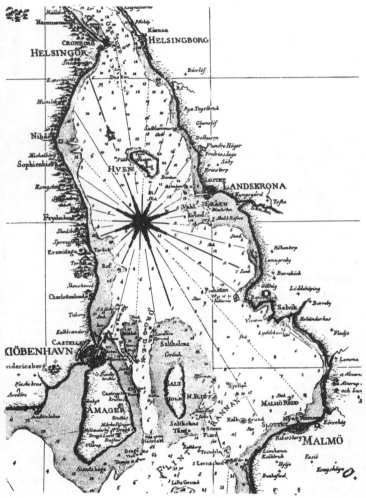

B

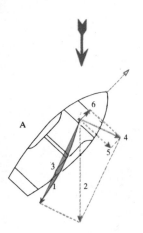 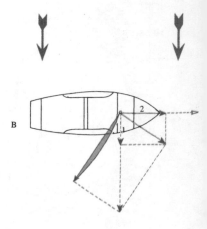

THEORY OF SAILING

A *A boat beating to windward*
1 Sail
2 The force and direction of the wind, which can be resolved into the two components, 3 and 4
3 This force blowing parallel to the sail may be disregarded
4 This force can be resolved into two components, 5 and 6
5 This force works abeam and tends to heel the boat and to drive it to leeward. This tendency, however, is largely overcome by the lateral resistance of the water on the boat's hull and keel.
6 Of the original wind force, it is this component only that carries the boat ahead.

B *Reaching; the wind abeam*
When the wind is abeam the lateral component (1) is reduced and the fore-and-aft component (2) is increased. The boat moves faster than when beating to windward (A).
C *Running*
When running, the sails must not be at right angles to the direction of the wind
1 Mainsail
2 Spinnaker

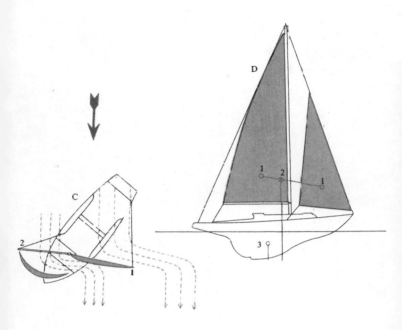

D *Center of effort*
   Every sail has a
   center of effort
   (1). The center of
   effort of the total
   sail area (2) is
   obtained by com-
   bining the cen-
   ters of each sail.
   Theoretically, if
   the center of
   effort is
   ahead of the cen-
   ter of lateral
   resistance (3),
   the boat will tend
   to pay off from
   the wind. If 2 is
   abaft 3, the boat
   will tend to come
   up into the wind.
   In reality, the
   boat, when sail-
   ing, is heeling to
   leeward and the
   force of the wind
   will be applied at
   the center of
   effort on the lee
   side of the boat
   and cause
   her to luff.
   To counteract
   this, the center of
   effort of the sails
   is always placed
   forward of the
   center of lateral
   resistance, as
   shown above.

241

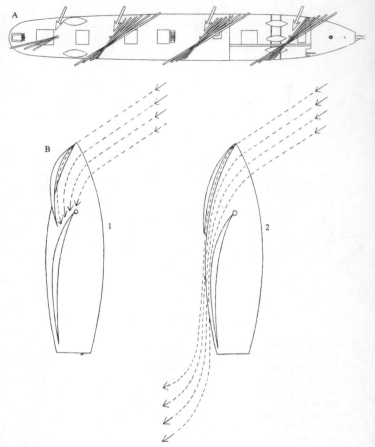

THE SET OF SAILS

A   *A square-rigged vessel beating to windward*
    In a square-rigger sailing on the wind the lower yards are always braced up more than the upper yards. The reason for this is that the lower sails cannot be set as flat as the upper sails, and thus require a broader wind to fill them than the small sails. Again, should the wind shift and the ship be caught aback, the upper sails will back first and warn the ship in time so that she can be paid off.

B   *The lead of the fore staysail sheet*
1   There must be sufficient gap between the fore staysail and the mainsail, otherwise (as in the figure) the driving force of the mainsail will be reduced

2   A fore staysail which is correctly sheeted increases the suction on the lee side of the mainsail and thus increases its power

C   *Unsteady wind*
A squall generally blows in a fan-shaped pattern. In spite of paying-off at the beginning and then luffing, the squall may be used to bring the boat to windward of her first track.

243

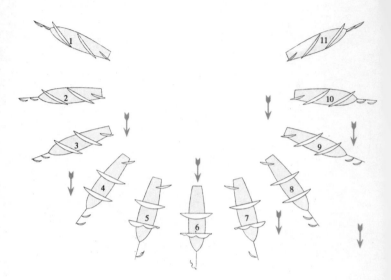

A BARK SAILING ON DIFFERENT COURSES

1 Bark sailing on the wind on the starboard tack
2 Sailing, reaching with wind abeam on the starboard side
3 Going large with the wind abaft the beam on the starboard side
4 Running free with the wind on the starboard quarter
5 Running before the wind; the wind is on the starboard side; headsails are partly blanketed, some staysails are furled

6 Running dead before the wind, scudding in a gale; spanker is furled, staysails not drawing, the headsails are blanketed
7 Running before the wind; wind is on the port side. Headsails are partly blanketed, some staysails are furled
8 Running free with the wind on the port quarter

9 Going large, sailing with a fair wind, with the wind abaft the beam on the port side
10 Sailing, reaching with the wind abeam on the port side
11 Sailing on the wind on the port tack

SMALL-BOAT HANDLING

To fetch a buoy
1 Sails set to the wind
2 Luff and trim sails to the wind
3 Luff and flatten in the sails

4 Luff as much as possible and spill the wind from the foresail and mainsail

5 Steer close to windward of the buoy and carefully judge the speed of approach

SMALL-BOAT HANDLING

A *Going about*
1 Keep her full and by
2 "Helm's alee"
3 Flatten the foresail (applicable to dull-turning boats only)
4 Haul the foresail over and trim sheets by the wind on the new tack

B *Jibing*
1 Boat steering before the wind; you want to take the wind on the port quarter
2 Luff a little and shorten your sheets
3 By ready to jibe
4 Up helm; jibe easily and let the sheets run
5 Meet her and trim yaw sails

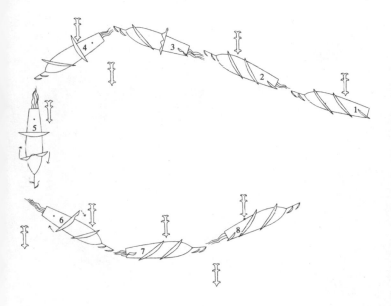

A SQUARE-RIGGED VESSEL, A THREE-MASTED BARK, WEARING

1 The bark is sailing on the wind on the starboard tack.

2 "Ready to wear ship!" The mainsail is clewed up and the braces are coiled down for running.

3 The spanker is furled. "Up helm!" "Square in the mainyard!" The wheel is put to port and the mainyard is squared.

4 Without sail aft the vessel is paying off.

5 The bark is before the wind. "Round forward!" The headsails are braced around and the jibs sheeted over to starboard.

6 When she is coming up on the new tack the headsails will meet her. The after yards are braced up.

7 The spanker is set and all sails are trimmed by the wind.

8 The bark is kept on the wind on the port tack. The main sail is set and the deck cleared up.

247

TACKING

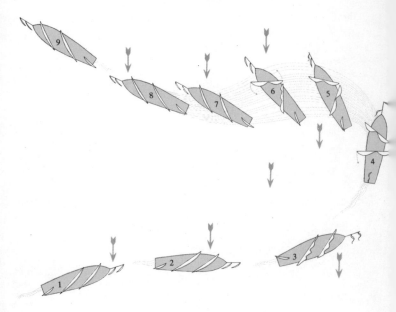

A SQUARE-RIGGED VESSEL, A THREE-MASTED BARK, TACKING

1 The bark is sailing on the wind on the port tack. "Ready about!"

2 She is kept off a little to make all sails draw better to increase the speed.

3 "Helm's alee!" The wheel is put down, the headsheets are let go to make the jibs spill the wind; the spanker is hauled aweather to assist the luffing.

4 The bark is nearly into the wind. Now "Mainsail haul!" The mainyards are braced around, the jibs are hauled over and sheeted home, while the vessel is head in the wind.

5 The movement ahead is decreasing. With the headsails aback the bark is forced over to port.

6 When the sails of the mainmast begin to fill, the order is, "Let go and haul!" and the headsails are hauled around.

7 The vessel is paying off until the sails are filling. All sails are trimmed by the wind.

8 The bark is going ahead, the wake is becoming normal.

9 She is kept on the wind on the starboard tack; the running gear is coiled down.

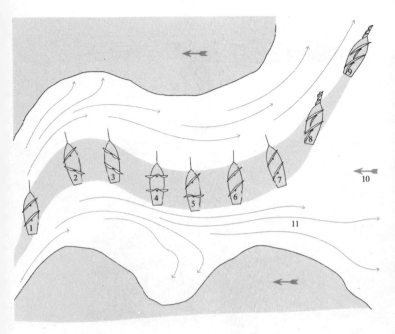

A SAILING VESSEL, A BRIG, BACKING AND FILLING DOWN A RIVER WITH THE
EBB TIDE, AGAINST A HEADWIND. SHE HAS ONLY THE TOPSAILS SET.

1 The brig is filling both topsails to make her move ahead to keep her in the fairway.
2 Backing the mainyard stops her progress and makes her drift broadside downriver.
3 Backing all makes her take a stern board.
4 By pointing the yards into the wind she is made to stand still and drift with the ebb tide.
5 Filling the fore topsail makes her draw ahead.
6 Filling all makes her go ahead more.
7 She is kept off a little to increase her movement through the water.
8 She is making sail, and trims them by the wind.
9 She is clear of the river and stands to sea under all sail on the starboard tack.
10 Wind direction
11 The ebb tide

249

TO HEAVE TO AND TO GOOSE-WING A SAIL

When a sailing ship was in a contrary gale of wind the order to heave to meant that most of sails were taken in and the helm was put down. This kept the ship's head to the wind, and, with the sea on the bow, she would ride well enough as long as some sail could be carried. This full-rigged ship has the fore topmast staysail and the goose-winged main lower topsail set. To furl the weather half of a lower topsail was the last resource to shorten sail without having to furl all and drift under bare poles. The large scale drawing shows a part of the main mast with the goose-winged lower topsail. The numbers indicate:

1 Main mast
2 Heel of topmast
3 Mainyard with mainsail furled
4 Upper topsail yard with topsail furled
5 Lower topsail yard
6 Goose-winged lower topsail
7 Heavy lashing on sail, parceled to protect sail from chafe
8 Size of lower topsail when set
9 Lower topsail buntlines
10 Lower topsail clewlines

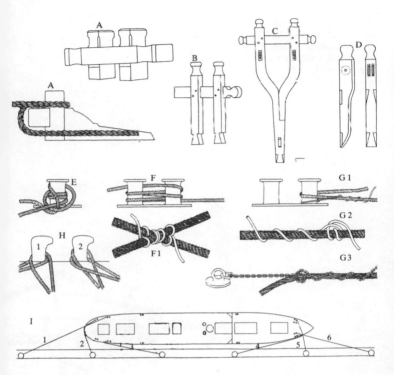

MOORING AND BELAYING

A *Bitts*
B *Knightheads*
C *Bitts on the forecastle head*
D *Knighthead*
  A-D are from a book on ship building by Å.C. Rålamb (1691)
E *Belaying to a single bollard*
F *Belaying to twin bollards*
  1 Racked turns
G *Stoppering a rope*
  Stoppers are used when hawsers are to be moved from the

winch to the bollards, chain stoppers are used on wires

H *Two berthing hawsers on the same bollard on shore*
  1 Wrong way, the second hawser will block the first one
  2 Right way, either of the hawsers can be removed from the bollard independently of the other

I *Berthing hawsers*
  1 Stern rope
  2 After breast rope
  3 After back spring
  4 Fore back spring
  5 Fore breast rope
  6 Head rope

251

This picture of a rope-yard is taken from the classic nautical volume *Allgemeines Wörterbuch der Marine* by J.H. Röding, published in 1798.

Index

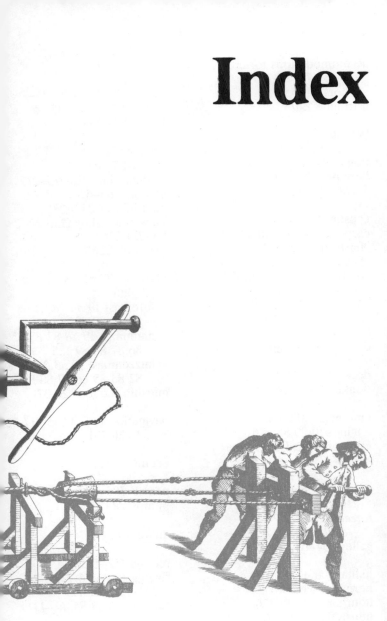